Twayne's English Authors Series

Sylvia E. Bowman, *Editor*

INDIANA UNIVERSITY

Arnold Wesker

(TEAS) 28

Arnold Wesker

By HAROLD U. RIBALOW

Twayne Publishers, Inc. :: New York

For my wife, SHOSHANA
Who enriches my life each day
And who plays a greater role than
She imagines in each book I write

Preface

In his study of the new British drama, John Russell Taylor observes that "Arnold Wesker has acquired a greater reputation on the strength of a still relatively smaller body of work than any other dramatist of his generation." [1] Mr. Taylor means, of course, in Great Britain; for in the early 1960's Arnold Wesker is not so well known in the United States as he is in England, although two of his dramas and a film version of a third have been performed in this country. It is obvious, however, that Wesker is a major figure in contemporary theater history.

Wesker, who is in his early thirties, [2] is the author of five published and produced plays, as well as two dramas completed but not yet staged at this writing. Three are known as the Wesker Trilogy: *Chicken Soup with Barley; Roots;* and *I'm Talking About Jerusalem.* When the Trilogy was presented as a consecutive unit on the London stage in 1960, Wesker became nationally famous. His earlier play, *The Kitchen,* was revived in 1961; and his 1962 drama, *Chips with Everything,* was a critical and commercial success in London. It toured the provinces and was imported to the New York stage in October, 1963. *Chips with Everything,* which had been named the best play of the year by the London critics, earned equally warm praise in New York and received favorable notices from every theater critic in the city.

Roots, the middle play of the Wesker Trilogy, was seen by playgoers in New York City in an off-Broadway production in 1961. [3] It received mixed reviews. I suspect that *Roots* in New York lacked the power of the London production because the brilliant actress, Joan Plowright, did not make the ocean voyage in order to undertake the role of Beatie Bryant.

The Kitchen, as a film, was shown in the United States in 1961 and 1962. Like *Roots,* it earned a respectful hearing, but Wesker clearly did not make the same impact with *The Kitchen* that he did in his native land. "It was a bad film; the play was much better," [4] Wesker has said.

Chips with Everything was imported with a cast of English players and Wesker told me that "The opening night performance was the best job this company has ever done." [5] Perhaps this is why *Chips with Everything* impressed the New York reviewers. It is a play without a woman on stage, without romance, without a "name" star; and yet it caught hold. It is a tribute to Arnold Wesker's growing maturity as a playwright.

Late in 1964 Wesker completed another long drama, entitled *Their Very Own and Golden City*, which is concerned with the growing influence of the Labour Party in Great Britain and the corruption of its leaders. Early in 1965 he wrote still another play, *The Four Seasons*, in which a man and a woman are the only two characters on stage, and the relationship between the sexes is probed throughout one long continuous act.

Yet Wesker himself stated—before he wrote his as-yet-unproduced new plays—"I personally think it is a little too soon to start writing a critical book on me." [6] After all, the bulk of his work still lies in the future.

Why, then, should a book be written about Wesker at this stage of his career? There is, I believe, a good reason for such a study now. Unlike other young writers, Arnold Wesker has a vision of what life should be like. He speaks for an entire generation of British working-class people. He is politically aware. He is not an "entertainer," but a playwright with a mission. And if he feels that he cannot project his message in his dramas alone, he has gone beyond the theater to organize a cultural movement known as Centre 42, which has the support of Britain's Trades Union Congress and scores of outstanding personalities in Great Britain and elsewhere. Wesker is a committed writer, one who is not interested in royalties alone, Hollywood, or a swimming pool in his backyard. He has marched in Ban-the-Bomb demonstrations and has sat in jail for his convictions, together, of course, with other distinguished Englishmen, including Lord Bertrand Russell.

Wesker represents, more than most, the "angry young men" of England. In 1956 John Osborne, in *Look Back in Anger*, exploded on the British scene and brought to the attention of the upper classes and the Establishment that it was possible to put on the English stage a play which articulates the anger and bitterness and frustration of the Englishman who cannot fit or be fitted into the "higher" classes. Wesker was deeply influenced by Osborne, but has drawn from his own East End Jewish, left-wing, Socialist background the essential material of his own rebellion. British critics have stated that *Chips with Everything* is a far more brilliant, eloquent denunciation of the Establishment than *Look Back in Anger.*[7] The student has surpassed the master.

John Russell Taylor, in writing of the Wesker Trilogy, says that

the most striking thing about Wesker . . . is the boldness of his concepts. The very idea of a trilogy attempting to sum up the situation of the working classes today (and glancing back as far as 1936 for the root causes of their present situation) is extraordinary enough in the modern theatre, but that it should have been carried out, that the plays should have been performed not only singly but together in repertory at a West End theatre, and that the whole thing should have been adjudged a success by most of the country's leading theatre critics is a striking achievement indeed.[8]

My purpose in this study is to clarify Wesker's plays within the patterns of recent British social, cultural, and literary trends, and to analyze his characters and themes, for both are central to his vision. The Centre 42 movement, a major development in contemporary British life, is vital not only to Wesker, who directs it and has been its founder, but to an entire generation of Englishmen and to the British working people as a whole. Therefore I describe in detail the origins of the movement and how it is accepted by the very people for whom it is intended. Wesker has been helpful to me because he has sent me the manuscripts of *Their Very Own and Golden City* and *The Four Seasons* in their first drafts so that I might be able to read them and include them in the body of his work, even though they have not as yet been staged. He also has sent me some of his essays and fugitive pieces which cannot be obtained in this country and he has talked with me at length, has corresponded generously and candidly, and has answered all my questions about his life and his work.

In addition to being an important British playwright, Wesker is one of a growing group of Jewish writers in England who are moving to the forefront of the British cultural scene.[9] His own plays are peopled with Jewish characters and he has lectured and written on his Jewish origins. Therefore, in discussing Wesker's plays and themes, I also point to his leadership as a Jewish writer.

Thus far, there has not been a single full-length study of the works of Arnold Wesker, although he has been the subject of scores of articles in popular, scholarly, and critical journals; and chapters have been devoted to him in volumes on modern British writing and on the drama. Each of his plays warrants analysis and the Wesker Trilogy, as a unit, deserves special attention. Through his dramas, his leadership of Centre 42, and his willingness to speak out on controversial and critical political and social issues, Wesker is a most important Englishman. We, who are interested in the creative act, in men touched by talent and with a vision of a better life for all men, should know this playwright.

Harold U. Ribalow

Acknowledgments

I am particularly grateful to Arnold Wesker for his cooperation in this work. He has given me permission to quote from his plays; he has sent me two new plays as yet unproduced; he has checked the facts in this manuscript; and he has talked with me at length about his ideas and his plans. He obtained for me British editions of books not available in this country and has helped me in every possible way. This is not an "authorized" study, nor has Wesker questioned my right to my views about his work. Nevertheless, this book would have had less value than it has had I not had the benefit of his own views and opinions.

Tom Maschler of Jonathan Cape, Wesker's British publisher, and Random House, Wesker's American publisher, have graciously permitted me to quote what I need from Wesker's plays, and John Russell Taylor, the British critic, and Henry Hewes, the American critic, have gone out of their way to be helpful to me.

The reader will notice that I have drawn material for this study from various sources: books, magazine articles, and newspapers. For permission to quote both brief and long passages, I wish to acknowledge my thanks to the following:

Plays and Players for:

"Working with Arnold" (April, 1962) and "Chips and Devotion" (December, 1962), interviews with John Dexter, by Peter Roberts.

Faber and Faber, Ltd. for:

Mid-Century Drama by Laurence Kitchin.

The London Magazine for:

"Culture With Chips," by Frank McGuinness (July, 1962). "Chicken Soup with Barley," by Sandro D'Amico (October, 1963).

The Twentieth Century for:
"Plays and Politics," by Richard Findlater (September, 1960).
"Art Is Not Enough," by Arnold Wesker (February, 1961).
Richard Findlater for:
"Plays and Politics," *The Twentieth Century* (September, 1960).
University of California Press for:
Postwar British Fiction by James Gindin.
The Critical Quarterly and A. R. Jones for:
"The Theatre of Arnold Wesker," by A. R. Jones (Winter, 1960).
Queen for:
"Chips with Everything," by Clancy Sigal (May 15, 1962).
The Observer for:
Kenneth Tynan's review of *Chips with Everything* (May 6, 1962).
New Statesman for:
"A World of Kitchens," by V. S. Pritchett (July 7, 1961).
"Chips and After," by Roger Gellert (May 11, 1962).
Commentary and the American Jewish Committee for:
"Jewish Writers in England," by Henry Popkin (February, 1961).
Harcourt, Brace and World, Inc. for:
A State of England, by Anthony Hartley.
The Reporter and John Rosselli for:
"The Wesker Twist," by John Rosselli (September 13, 1962. Copyright 1962 by The Reporter Magazine Company).
Jewish Observer and Middle East Review for:
"Arnold Wesker: Is Sincerity Enough?," by Renee Winegarten (April 19, 1963).
The Spectator for:
"Chips with Everything," by Bamber Gascoigne (May 11, 1962).
"Not Talking About Jerusalem," by Kingsley Amis (August 10, 1962).
Robert Hatch for:
"Theatre," *The Nation* (March 25, 1961).
"Arise, Ye Playgoers of the World," *Horizon* (July, 1961).

Acknowledgments

New Theatre Magazine, published by the Department of Drama, University of Bristol for:
"Question and Answer," an interview with Arnold Wesker by Jill Pomerance (April, 1960).
John Russell Taylor for:
Anger and After
"Mr. Wesker's 'Menace,'" *The Listener* (December 12, 1963).
'Arnold Wesker," *The Times* (London) (December 12, 1963).
The Jewish Quarterly for:
"Anglo Jewish Literature," by Joseph Leftwich (Spring, 1953).
"The Young Writer and the Theatre," by Bernard Kops (Summer, 1953).
"Trends in Anglo-Jewish Writing," by Gerda Charles (Spring, 1963).

Contents

Chronology

1932   Arnold Wesker born in Stepney, London's East End, on May 24, to Joseph Wesker, a Russian-Jewish tailor, and Hungarian-born Leah (Perlmutter) Wesker, who frequently supported the family by working in kitchens.

1939-
1945   During the War, Arnold was sent out of London as an evacué and for six years lived with foster parents in various sections of England and Wales. Wesker missed London, and always returned when he had the opportunity. Thus, for two thirds of the time he was in London.

1943   Attended Upton House School in Hackney in London's East End, where he was trained in bookkeeping, typing, and shorthand.

1945   He was attracted to the stage while still in school, and joined an amateur acting group.

1948-
1950   Worked at a wide variety of jobs. He was a furniture maker's apprentice, a carpenter's mate, and a bookseller's assistant.

1950   Entered the Royal Air Force, where he did nothing of military significance. He did, however, organize a dramatic group for enlisted airmen and, of course, a dozen years later wrote a play based on his Royal Air Force experiences.

1952-
1956   Discharged from the Royal Air Force and accepted whatever work he could find. He worked as a plumber's mate, a farm laborer's seed porter, and a kitchen porter before he found a profession as a pastry cook. He worked as a pastry cook for two years in London and as a chef for nine months in Paris. He saved enough money to enter the London School of Film Technique. Outside its National Film Theatre one evening, he met Lindsay Anderson and showed

Anderson *Pools,* a short story which Wesker hoped could be made into a film. Nothing came of this, but Anderson read *The Kitchen* and *Chicken Soup with Barley* and brought Wesker to the notice of George Devine of the Royal Court Theatre in London. Anderson had sent the script of *Chicken Soup with Barley* to Devine, who passed it along to the Belgrade Theatre in Coventry, where it was produced on July 7, under the direction of John Dexter.

1958 The Arts Council of Great Britain, under a scheme for assisting promising new playwrights, awarded Wesker £300. By this time he had completed *Chicken Soup with Barley.*

1958 Married, on November 14, Doreen Cecile Bicker, whom he met when she was a waitress at a Norwich hotel. They are the parents of three children, two sons and a daughter.

1958 *Pools,* a short story, which also had been written as a film script, published in *The Jewish Quarterly* (Winter, 1958-1959).

1959 *Roots* produced at the Belgrade Theatre in Coventry on May 25, directed by John Dexter.

1959 *Chicken Soup with Barley* and *Roots* published in Penguin editions.

1959 Wesker was winner of London *Evening Standard* award as the most promising British dramatist of the year.

1959 *The Kitchen* produced at the Royal Court Theatre in London on September 13 by the English Stage Society, under the direction of John Dexter.

1959 "Time Parts the Memory," a poem, published in *The Jewish Quarterly* (Winter, 1959-60).

1960 *I'm Talking About Jerusalem* opened at the Belgrade Theatre in Coventry on April 4.

1960 Enormous impact made when three plays, known as the Wesker Trilogy, were produced in their entirety at the Royal Court Theatre in London. *Chicken Soup with Barley* opened on June 7; *Roots* on June 28; *I'm Talking About Jerusalem* on July 27.

1960 *I'm Talking About Jerusalem* published in a Penguin edition; also *The Kitchen,* in Penguin's *New English Dramatists 2.*

1960   *The Wesker Trilogy,* including all three dramas performed in London in the summer, published in a single volume by Jonathan Cape.

1961   *Roots,* the first of Wesker's plays to be produced in the United States, shown off Broadway at the Mayfair Theatre in New York City on March 6, won wide, but mixed, notices.

1961   *The Kitchen* revived on June 27, at the Royal Court Theatre in London.

1961   A film version of *The Kitchen* released in the United States; played in art threaters around the country.

1961   Wesker played a leading role in demonstrations against the use of nuclear weapons and, together with Bertrand Russell and other notable Englishmen, was sentenced to a month in prison.

1961   *The Wesker Trilogy* published by Random House in New York.

1961   *The Kitchen* published in a revised edition by Jonathan Cape and by Random House.

1961   Wesker director of Centre 42, a cultural movement for popularizing the arts, primarily through trade union support and participation, which gained the active support of important, influential Englishmen in all walks of life.

1962   *Chips with Everything,* directed by John Dexter, opened at the Royal Court Theatre in London on April 27; subsequently transferred to the West End, becoming Wesker's first West End hit. Voted the best play of 1962 after it opened at the Vaudeville on the Strand. Also opened in Sheffield and Glasgow a few days after the London opening, thereby setting a precedent for new plays to be opened in the provinces instead of waiting years for the run in the metropolis to finish.

1962   Wesker's essay, "The Secret Reins" published in *Encounter* (March, 1962), explains the history of the Centre 42 movement and its importance to him as its founder.

1963   *The Menace,* an original television play, in its first draft, published in *The Jewish Quarterly* (Spring, 1963).

1963   *Chips with Everything,* Wesker's second play to be seen in the United States, opened on October 1, at the Plymouth

Theatre. Wesker made his first visit to the United States a week prior to the play's opening and left a week later.

1963 *Chips with Everything*, as one of the outstanding plays of 1962, published in *New English Dramatists 7*, in a Penguin edition, together with David Rudkin's *Afore Night Come* and Giles Cooper's *Everything in the Garden*.

1963 *Chips with Everything* published in its entirety, plus short feature on the playwright, in *Theatre Arts* (October).

1963 *Menace* first shown on television, December 8, in the British Broadcasting Company's "First Night" series.

1964 *Chips with Everything* closed on Broadway on February 8, after a run of 149 performances.

1964 Wesker's article, "Art—Therapy or Experience," published in *Views No. 4* (Spring, 1964).

1964 *The Wesker Trilogy* published in a Penguin edition.

1964 *The Kitchen* published in a volume of Penguin Plays, with *Epitaph for George Dillon* by John Osborne and Anthony Creighton and *The Hamlet of Stepney Green* by Bernard Kops.

1964 *Roots* included in *The New British Drama*, edited by Henry Popkin, published by Grove Press.

1964 *Chips with Everything* included in *The Best Plays 1963-1964*, edited by Henry Hewes, published by Dodd, Mead.

1964 Wrote *Their Very Own and Golden City*.

1965 First draft of *The Four Seasons* completed January 18.

CHAPTER 1

Wesker and the New British Drama

WHEN John Osborne's *Look Back in Anger* opened in London on May 8, 1956, the English stage was revolutionized. For the first time the British were faced with characters—on the stage—hitherto strange to them. Moreover, they were exposed to viewpoints that were disturbing to them. Many British critics have written at length on this phenomenon.[1]

This transformation has not yet been recognized by American audiences, for few of the new plays have been performed in this country. But in the United States the introduction of the "angry young men," a phrase heavily overused, has been made forceful in other media, particularly in novels, short stories, and films; and some of the novels and stories have been made into the harshly realistic British films that have attracted and won the admiration of Americans.

Of course, English novelists always have been popular in the United States, but I am not thinking of the more formal writers, like Ivy Compton-Burnett, C. P. Snow, L. P. Hartley, or even the oddly original Muriel Spark. Within the past half dozen or so years, we have been reading with increasing interest the vigorous fiction of Englishmen who fight the Establishment; who write, not of Oxford and Cambridge, but of the aggressive Yorkshireman marrying the daughter of a rich businessman and moving upward in society; the Borstal boy, or delinquent; the athlete who bleeds for his money; the man who takes his women casually and betrays them with equal indifference; the working-class young man who is willing to take a battering for his married mistress; the women who hate to be enslaved by their sexuality.

John Braine's Joe Lampton, in *Room at the Top* and *Life at the Top*, is typical of the new hero of British fiction. He marries the boss's daughter, although he loves a married woman. He makes his way forward, not through his business ability, but because he makes pregnant a girl whose father can help him get ahead. In *Life at the Top* Braine shows us that he is not unaware of the dangers of such "success." Joe Lampton, in the end, is a trapped man. He has gone ahead, but at the loss of his dignity and individuality. In John Wain's *Hurry on Down*, Charles Lumley also rebels against the patterns of his society. He fights hard, but finally he also succumbs to the material comforts of a good job in television.

Alan Sillitoe, author of *Saturday Night and Sunday Morning* and *Key to the Door*, concerns himself with the Seatons; and Arthur, in the first of the two books, like Wain's hero, struggles to express himself as an individual. But he also loses out and is preparing at the conclusion of the novel to work hard in order to make a successful marriage with a girl who seeks middle-class conformity and propriety. Yet in Sillitoe's short story, "The Loneliness of the Long Distance Runner," the Borstal boy hero manages to reject conformity. He can win an important race for his institution but deliberately turns away from victory in a gesture of defiance.

In Doris Lessing's impressive and vast novel, *The Golden Notebook*, women who consider themselves "free women" discover that they cannot do without love; no matter how hard they battle for independence, they are dependent on men, on sexual satisfaction, on orgasm. Yet in John Harvey's *Within and Without*, a novel told by a man from his viewpoint, man is as trapped as woman. The hero loves a girl whom he betrays and leaves for a girl who can help him get ahead. One understands Miss Lessing's bitterness and Sillitoe's rebelliousness more clearly when one reads Harvey's little novel, which is unknown in the United States.

David Storey, author of *This Sporting Life*, *Flight into Camden*, and *Radcliffe*, writes of rugby players, a woman who takes up with a married man, and a homosexual relationship, and he handles his themes with power and sensitivity. He produces strong prose and vivid scenes. He treats cruelty and human relationships seldom approached by the more "cultured" and subtle writers like C. P. Snow, who is sophisticated but bloodless.

These fiction writers have crossed the ocean and have made a strong impression in the United States. And British films, many of them made from some of the previously listed novels and stories, have made us aware of England's new social writers. We have seen in this country realistic films based on Sillitoe's *Saturday Night and Sunday Morning* and *The Loneliness of the Long Distance Runner;* on Braine's *Room at the Top;* on Storey's *This Sporting Life.* Remarkable films have been made which demonstrate England's seamier side: *A Taste of Honey; A Kind of Loving; Expresso Bongo; The L-Shaped Room;* and almost a score of others, including *Look Back in Anger.*[2] These films have influenced American movie-making and have forced Americans to the realization that England is not necessarily a country of the gentry and upper-class people.

I   *Dramas of the Working Class*

The drama in England has undergone an even greater transformation. John Russell Taylor, who has analyzed the situation closely, has written:

Not all the plays which have emerged have been good, of course, or even interesting, and the mere fact that a playwright is under forty can hardly be regarded as a guarantee of quality by even the most optimistic. But there is a hard core of exciting new writing in the theatre, almost entirely from writers under forty, and quite often from writers under thirty. They have, moreover, two further distinguishing features: their tremendous variety and patent unwillingness to fall neatly behind one standard or one leader; and the fact that the great majority of them have working-class origins.[3]

This is the big surprise: that they are men and women from a society previously not heard from. They include Arnold Wesker and Harold Pinter, as well as John Osborne; Shelagh Delaney and Doris Lessing; Alun Lewis and Clive Exton; Ann Jellicoe and Bernard Kops.

Taylor has stressed it in this way:

For many years the West End stage has been a middle-class preserve: middle-class writers, more often than not university educated, have written for mainly middle-class audiences. But now things are different. Few of the new writers have been to university—John Arden and John Mortimer are exceptional in this respect—though whether they could any of them hope to escape the university net were they aged about ten is now another matter. Arnold Wesker is the son of a Jewish tailor in the East End, and Harold Pinter, too, comes from an East End Jewish family; Shelagh Delaney, as all the world knows, comes from Salford and did not even manage to scrape into the local grammar school; Alun Lewis is Liverpool-Welsh, an ex-Bevin boy turned straight-man to music-hall comics at the time he wrote his first play; he and several others, John Osborne, Clive Exton, and Harold Pinter among them, have worked their way up from the ranks, as it were, after periods spent with varying degrees of success as humble repertory actors.[4]

The English Stage Company at the Royal Court Theatre put on many of the plays of these new dramatists. Joan Littlewood, who ran the Theatre Workshop at Stratford, introduced Delaney and Brendan Behan. The British audiences were intrigued with plays like *A Taste of Honey*, which deals with a girl who has a child by a Negro and is befriended by a homosexual; *Look Back in Anger*, about rebellious Jimmy Porter who is tough and casual with his women; *The Caretaker* by Pinter, which is a strange, symbolic play about a tramp who invades the private lives of two brothers. The theater had suddenly come alive with new personalities, new themes, new viewpoints.

At first *Look Back in Anger* was not a critical success, but it soon attracted those British audiences who, at first, had looked upon it strangely, if not with anger. Kenneth Tynan said, "I agree that *Look Back in Anger* is likely to remain a minority taste. What matters, however, is the size of the minority. I estimate it at roughly 6,733,000, which is the number of people in this country between twenty and thirty. . . . I doubt if I could love anyone who did not wish to see *Look Back in Anger*. It is the best young play of its decade." [5]

But the real impact of this new theater was made when *Roots* by Wesker was a critical success, due in some measure to the performance of Joan Plowright who, in addition to her vivid interpretation of the leading role of Beatie Bryant, was an actress of international reputation. The new dramatists were now accepted. Pinter became a television regular, as did Clive Exton; Alun Owen turned to radio. Delaney's play was a startling one and turned into an American hit and a popular film. Osborne himself continued to write intriguing scripts and remained in the public eye. But it was with Wesker and his trilogy of the Kahn family, performed in the summer of 1960 in London, that the new dramatists came of age.

II *Education and Background*

Arnold Wesker is the son of Joseph Wesker, a Russian-Jewish tailor, and Leah (Perlmutter) Wesker. In his plays and in interviews Wesker has written and spoken of the closeness of his family ties. Yet during World War II, he was evacuated from London to the country and lived with foster parents in England and Wales. He has been quoted as saying, "I never stopped longing to get back to London, bombs or no bombs. My childhood was poor but happy. I come from pretty earthy folks. We are a close family." [6] He has not written about his life as an evacué, but an excellent picture of this kind of living can be obtained from the autobiography of Bernard Kops, *The World Is a Wedding*, for Kops, from the same background as Wesker, also was evacuated and lived with foster parents.

Wesker's education was by no means of the middle or upper-class kind. He attended Jewish schools and three elementary schools in Stepney and Hackney, both in the East End. He was attracted to acting, although he had studied bookkeeping, typing, and shorthand. He joined the Habonim, a Zionist youth group, and performed in a pageant. But his schooling was brief, and he took on whatever odd jobs he could find. He was an apprentice to a furniture maker, and then a bookseller's assistant and a carpenter's mate before he went into the Royal Air Force. Wesker remembers "cleaning dustbins" in the Royal Air Force, but it is apparent from his *Chips with Everything* that he noticed a great deal of Royal Air Force life and its conflicts and eventually put his service experience to artistic use.

When he was discharged from the Royal Air Force in 1952 he was a man in search of himself and an opportunity to earn a living. He wrote a novel under the D. H. Lawrence influence, but it was not a good book and has never been published. He accepted jobs: as a plumber's mate, a farm laborer's seed porter, a kitchen porter, and, finally, as a pastry cook. He worked in France and England at this latter job, and *The Kitchen* was drawn from his experiences in various kitchens. Ronnie Kahn, who is Arnold Wesker in the trilogy, has a rather eloquent hatred for kitchens.

While he was in the Royal Air Force Wesker had some opportunities to act and, following his Royal Air Force career, he entered the London School of Film Technique. There he was introduced to the work of Lindsay Anderson and the Free Cinema Movement and other young men who were training themselves to write film documentaries. "I owe a particular debt to Lindsay Anderson," Wesker has stated. "I recognized in his writings something which I was trying to do, to affirm something I felt which was in contradiction to the mood of the time, its cynicism, despair, and disillusion." [7]

It was Lindsay Anderson who brought *Chicken Soup with Barley* to the "right" theater people, and eventually Tony Richardson agreed to try the play in Coventry. *Chicken Soup with Barley* was offered at the Belgrade Theatre on July 7, 1958. Wesker won an Arts Council grant of £300 and half of an Encyclopaedia Britannica play prize and thus he became a serious playwright, working on film scripts and continuing to create his trilogy. *Roots* was performed for the first time at the Belgrade Theatre on May 25, 1959, and the critics started to take serious notice of him. Wesker received the London *Evening Standard* award of that year as the most promising British playwright of 1959. On April 4, 1960, *I'm Talking About Jerusalem*, the concluding play in the trilogy, opened at the Belgrade Theatre, and later that summer all three plays were produced at the Royal Court Theatre in London. It was the first time in the memory of any Londoner that a contemporary dramatist was presenting three plays within six weeks on a London stage. Quite naturally, Wesker became famous, and his name was now being mentioned in the United States as well. In March, 1961, *Roots* was exported to this country for an off-Broadway production (at the Mayfair Theatre on March 6, 1961).

Chips with Everything also has played in England and the United States, and *The Kitchen* has been seen on both continents. *The Kitchen* first opened at the Royal Court Theatre on September 13, 1959, and was revived in a revised version on June 27, 1961. The film of *The Kitchen* was shown in the United States in 1961. *Chips with Everything* opened on April 27, 1962, at the

Royal Court Theatre, but was soon transferred to the West End and has since played in many English cities. It was offered to American audiences on October 1, 1963, and ran until February 8, 1964, closing after 149 performances.

But Wesker has been more than a prolific and successful playwright. He was the motivating force behind the Centre 42 movement; he participated in British Ban-the-Bomb demonstrations and was sentenced to a month in jail in September, 1961.

Wesker is the most socially-minded of all the new English dramatists; while Harold Pinter has captured the imagination of the nonsocial critics, Wesker is more warmly debated and discussed in England than any other contemporary British dramatist. The chapters that follow will, I hope, demonstrate why this is so.

CHAPTER 2

The Kitchen

ONE of Wesker's earliest plays, *The Kitchen*, also is one of his slightest. It has, however, had a variety of lives. Entered for the *Observer* Play Competition in 1957, it failed to win a prize and was shelved until Wesker met Lindsay Anderson. Eventually it was produced at the Royal Court Theatre in 1959. In 1961 a film version of *The Kitchen* was shown in England and the United States. In the same year *The Kitchen*, expanded and revised, was revived at the Royal Court Theatre.

The Kitchen reads far less well than it plays. The entire drama takes place in the kitchen of a large London restaurant. Wesker's skill helps to capture the intensity and frenzy of the workers who have to prepare and serve thousands of meals a day. But even here, in so early a play of his, Wesker is indulging in symbolism. Much of the dialogue makes little impact on the reader; yet on stage the play moves the spectators. What makes *The Kitchen* at all memorable is that Wesker sees in his men and women the people of the world, with their dreams, their conflicts, their loves, their hates, their inability to get along together. Behind the daily grubby work there is a message. Men struggle without knowing why. They grope for love, which, more often than not, passes them by.

In a lengthy Introduction and Notes for the Producer Wesker explains the scene and purpose of the play. "This," he tells us, "is a play about a large kitchen called the Tivoli. All kitchens, especially during service, go insane. There is the rush, there are the petty quarrels, grumbles, false prides, and snobbery. Kitchen staff instinctively hate dining-room staff, and all of them hate the customer. He is the personal enemy." [1] Wesker, who himself worked in kitchens for four years and was a pastry cook, knows his milieu and captures the life of the kitchen and the people who inhabit it, work and sweat and fight in it. But he is interested in the kitchen for other reasons. "The world might have been a stage for Shakespeare," he writes, "but to me it is a kitchen, where people come and go and cannot stay long enough to understand each other, and friendships, loves and enmities are forgotten as quickly as they are made." [2]

I Demonstrating an Idea

"I am impatient," Wesker has told an interviewer,[3] "with two people who do nothing more than talk to each other on the stage. What I try to have them do is *demonstrate* an idea, live it out, act it out. In fact without being aware of it I think I've always strived for this demonstrating of the point rather than talking about it; and this is why, in the first play I wrote, *The Kitchen*, there are no long patches of argument and intellectual discussion. The whole play is an attempt to recreate the atmosphere of the Kitchen in order to demonstrate a particular point." [4]

John Russell Taylor describes the day on which Wesker focuses in *The Kitchen:* "The day is crowded, what with illicit love among the ladles, a knife fight, a scalding, a miscarriage, and a climactic smash-up, but it all has a purpose: it is to show what happens when people are cooped up, constantly frustrated and limited entirely to the dreariest, least stimulating practicalities." [5]

Not yet skilled in drawing character through dialogue or action, Wesker analyzes his main characters in a note to the producer. It is through these notes, rather than through stage action, that one gets to know the people on stage. This is, of course, a weakness; it makes the drama understandable to the reader, but not to the spectator.

The major character is Peter, a twenty-three-year-old German boy who has been working at the Tivoli for three years. He is in love with Monique, a waitress who has been his mistress but who refuses to leave her husband. She has been twice pregnant by Peter but lost both infants and is now pregnant again. Kevin, a new cook, a twenty-two-year-old Irishman, is bewildered by the pace in this kitchen. Raymond and Paul, pastry cooks, work together calmly. Paul is a Jew; Raymond, an Italian. Alfredo, a veteran chef of sixty-five, is the most rapid worker in the kitchen; independent, he is unwilling to impart information to anyone else.

The kitchen also has Cypriots, a German, and men from many countries. The staff members steal food, argue with one another, talk about women, and constantly complain about the owner of the restaurant, Mr. Marengo. It is a noisy, lively, tight little world.

Dimitri, a Cypriot kitchen porter, has made a portable radio and takes pride in it. Paul, the young Jew, commends him for his handiwork, and Raymond, marveling at the skill shown by Dimitri, asks him: "Why waste your time with dishes in this place? You can't get a job in a factory?" Dimitri replies, "A factory? You think I find happiness in a factory? . . . All day I would screw in knobs. I tell you, in a factory a man makes a little piece till he becomes a little piece, you know what I mean?" This attitude reminds one of Dave's philosophy in *I'm Talking About Jerusalem.* Dave, too, had turned his back on the mechanization which represses and suppresses modern man.

Nearly all of the men have their own private dreams. One wants to go to America; another wants as many new women as he can seduce; Peter dreams of marrying Monique. They all are amazed at Mr. Marengo's passion for his business, his desire to make his restaurant, his kitchen, the best around. Peter analyzes Marengo and castigates his way of life:

He is a man, he is a restaurant. I tell you. He goes to market at five thirty in the morning; returns here, reads the mail, goes up to the office and then comes down here to watch the service. Here he stands, sometimes he walks round touching the hot-plate, closing the hot-plate doors, then looking inside this thing and that thing. Till the last customer he stays. Then he has a sleep upstairs in his office. Half an hour after we come back, he is here again—till nine thirty, maybe ten at night. Every day, morning to night. What kind of a life is that, in a kitchen! Is that a life I ask you?

Kevin, the new man, complains that he has never worked so hard in his life. The customers are demanding; the waitresses rush about; the chefs are sour and nervous. He warns himself that he had better get out of this kind of life: "This is no place for a human being." But Dimitri laughs at him. He wonders why Kevin is grumbling. "Is different anywhere else?" he asks. "People come and people go, big excitement, big noise. What for? In the end who do you know? You make a friend, you going to be all you life his friend but when you go from here—pshtt! You forget!" Peter, symbolically comparing the kitchen to life itself, informs Kevin: "This—this madhouse, it's always here. When you go, when I go, when Dimitri go—this kitchen stays. It'll go on when we die, think about that. We work here—eight hours a day, and yet—it's nothing. We take nothing."

Paul is a thoughtful Jewish worker, and he tells his fellow workers, during a lull in the day's work, that man is thoughtless, unfeeling, unwilling to understand his neighbor. One of his own neighbors, a bus driver, had gone on strike and he, Paul, had sympathized with him, given him encouragement. But when there was a peace march on a Sunday, this same neighbor was bitter about it; he had said that he wished a bomb had been dropped on the marchers because the march was holding up traffic. "I don't want him to say I'm right," Paul explains, "I don't want him to agree with what I did, but what terrifies me is that he didn't stop to think that this man helped me in my cause so maybe, only *maybe*, there's something in my cause. . . . And the horror is this —that there's a wall, a big wall between me and millions of people like him. And I think—where will it end? What do you do about it?" And so the workers argue and debate and think and dream and find themselves as helpless in the world as they do in the kitchen.

Violence, however, is not far from the men. One is scalded. One of the pregnant women miscarries in the kitchen. Peter cannot get Monique to go away with him and she tells him that her husband is buying a new house and she will go off with him. Peter runs amok. He smashes the crockery and breaks the gas leads to the serving-counter. He cuts his hands and is covered with blood. The kitchen is in bedlam. For a moment the world of the kitchen is shattered; Mr. Marengo, the owner, is astonished by what he sees, and he does not understand any of it. "Why does everybody sabotage me?" he cries out. His cry is the call of a man puzzled by life and those who work for him: "I give work, I pay well, yes? They eat what they want, don't they? I don't know what more to give a man. He works, he eats, I give him money. This is life, isn't it? I haven't made a mistake, have I? I live in the right world, don't I?"

Mr. Marengo rushes about, looking with dismay at his wrecked kitchen. He stares at the bloodied Peter and calls out, "Maybe you can tell me something I don't know—just tell me." There is no answer. Mr. Marengo persists, "I want to learn something." He faces the kitchen and speaks to anyone, everyone, "Is there something I don't know? What more do you want? What is there more, tell me?" Peter shakes his head at his boss, gesturing that he cannot help Mr. Marengo; if Mr. Marengo doesn't know, he, Peter, cannot explain. And Mr. Marengo cries out, "What is there more? What is there more? What is there more?" as the curtain falls.

II *Microcosm of a World*

The Kitchen is a microcosm of the larger world, and Wesker asks the same questions here that he asks later in his longer, more ambitious dramas. His people change and are different, perhaps, but they live in the same unfeeling, puzzling world. Peter, unable to overcome the loss of Monique, cracks up in *The Kitchen.* Throughout Wesker's work, in the trilogy and in *Chips with Everything,* men and women are faced with situations which can crush them. Mainly, it is our society which is so overwhelming.

The Kitchen, to some critics, is not particularly realistic. For example, John Russell Taylor asks, "what sort of London restaurant serves 1,500 lunches in two hours every day, with waitress service and presumably a seating capacity of around 500?" [6] To this thrust, Wesker has a simple reply: "The answer to this is that there is no such kitchen in London, because the kitchen in mind was based on the one in Paris, to which *all* the facts apply." [7]

Yet these thrusts and parries beg the question. That *The Kitchen* is too melodramatic and is "so crude that it leans over uncomfortably far into the realm of farce" [8] may also be true. Moreover, Wesker himself has had second thoughts about *The Kitchen.* In an interview with Taylor he said, "And in *The Kitchen* I would not, if I were writing the play now, make Dimitri *say* that the kitchen is like the whole world. It's not that I've changed my mind about what I was trying to say . . . it's just that I think now I would say them in a different way, in a way which makes fuller use of the complex and subtle language the theatre puts at a writer's disposal." [9]

This statement, made by Wesker more than a half dozen years

after the writing of *The Kitchen,* indicates he may have become diffident about so early a work. Nevertheless, the questions he raises in *The Kitchen* ring in the mind; they require answers. *The Kitchen* does not answer them; but to pose the important questions is important in itself.

CHAPTER 3

Chicken Soup with Barley

A RNOLD WESKER'S three plays about the Kahn family con-
stitute a rather remarkable achievement on many levels which
will be considered in the chapters that follow. The first play in
the trilogy, which has come to be known as the Wesker Trilogy, is
Chicken Soup with Barley, first produced in 1958. *Roots* followed
a year later and *I'm Talking About Jerusalem* in 1960. In the summer of 1960 the entire trilogy was presented in London; thus far,
only *Roots* has been seen in the United States.

The trilogy does not follow any particular chronological form,
but each play impinges upon each other; the characters in the
dramas become clearer on second readings and one makes discov-
eries about them in a haphazard as well as a consecutive fashion.
The printed program for the Wesker Trilogy, issued by the English Stage Company, contains some pertinent material about the
entire project. "The three plays," according to the program, "although each is complete in itself, together form a trilogy. This is
in itself a unique achievement for a young playwright. Each of
the plays in its different way tackles social and political problems
of great importance, yet they are linked together with a common
human theme. The current presentation of the three plays as a
trilogy is an unusual event in the world of the theatre. Although
there are several examples of trilogies of books and films, there
have been few precedents for the Wesker Trilogy." [1]

I *Characters and Themes*

It is a curiosity that the trilogy, truly a single unified work, does
not have all of its characters appearing in each of the plays.
Chicken Soup with Barley introduces—in depth—Sarah and Harry
Kahn and their children Ada and Ronnie, as well as various relatives and friends. *Roots* is the story of Ronnie and his girl friend,

Beatie Bryant, but Ronnie is an off-stage figure. Although Beatie is constantly quoting him, the audience never sees him. *I'm Talking About Jerusalem* focuses on Ada and Dave Simmonds. Sarah and Ronnie appear in it. And *Chicken Soup with Barley* presents a great deal of material about Dave which is scarcely mentioned in *I'm Talking About Jerusalem*. Therefore, to get a rounded protrait of Dave, one must also be acquainted with *Chicken Soup with Barley*. Ronnie, who is a cook in Paris during part of the *Chicken Soup with Barley* story, is obviously Arnold Wesker himself. And the play *The Kitchen,* which is not part of the trilogy, is based on Wesker's (Ronnie's) experiences.

In a program note, Wesker condenses the meaning of his trilogy, stressing that "a number of themes bind the trilogy together. Basically, it is a family; on another level it is a play about human relationships; and on a third, and most important level, it is a story of people moved by political ideas in a particular social time." [2] Wesker points out that the plays deal with different theories of socialism. *Chicken Soup with Barley* "handles the Communist aspect." [3] *Roots* is concerned with the personal aspect, and *I'm Talking About Jerusalem* "is a sort of study in a William Morris kind of socialism." [4] The three plays catapulted Wesker to the forefront of the British stage, and the critics realized that they were dealing with an ambitious, passionate, idealistic writer. How they reacted and what judgments they made are treated in "The Critical View."

The Author's Note to *Chicken Soup with Barley,* brief but significant, reads, in its entirety: "*Chicken Soup with Barley* was not written as an anti-Soviet play and the author insists that no theatrical, film, television, or broadcasting company should present it as such. He would further remind all concerned that an indictment against the Inquisition is no more an attack on Christianity than the indictment based on recent Soviet admissions is an attack upon socialism. Let no mud be thrown; few people's hands are clean. Just let us think again." [5]

The Action

Chicken Soup with Barley begins in 1936 and ends in 1956. Much happens to the Kahn family in this two-decade period. Harry Kahn, the father, who at the outset is only thirty-five years old, "amiable but weak," goes into a physical decline. He suffers a stroke; by 1956 he has had a second and is sometimes senile. We learn in *I'm Talking About Jerusalem* of his rantings. His wife, Sarah, two years older than her husband, has vitality and energy. Hers is a warm but dominating personality. Unlike her weak husband, she is strongly political minded and is a convinced Communist. Yet the years also deal heavily with her. At the end she is lonesome and begs her son Ronnie not to leave her. Ronnie, only five years old in 1936, comes forward more strongly as the play progresses. One of the weaknesses of the Wesker Trilogy, however, is that Ronnie never takes the center of the stage. He is echoed in *Roots*, he has a few passages in *I'm Talking About Jerusalem*, and he flits about in *Chicken Soup with Barley*, but at no time does Wesker stop to study him at leisure. Ronnie, like Wesker, is the onlooker. Ada, a beautiful twenty-five-year-old girl, is something like her mother, argumentative, politically aware; she is in love with Dave Simmonds, who goes off to fight with the Loyalists in Spain.[6]

Chicken Soup with Barley, in its opening scenes, sets the stage not only for the later dramas in the trilogy, but also for the political and social atmosphere of the times. It is 1936, and Oswald Mosley's fascists are demonstrating for the Franco forces in Spain, while the working-class people are preparing a counter demonstration. Sarah and Harry nag at each other, and Dave and his friends discuss the possibility of volunteering for the war on the Loyalist side. Talk about socialism fills the air. British police violence is castigated. This is a lively family. They have ideals. They are close to the Communist movement. They are aware of the conflicts of the day. True, Sarah isn't happy with Harry, but it is a family.

In the second act, ten years later, matters haven't changed much. Sarah still nags her husband; Harry, weak and unaggressive, cannot handle his energetic wife. Ronnie, who has now grown up, hands out pamphlets for a May Day parade. Ada is waiting for Dave, now her husband, to return from war service overseas. She hasn't seen much of him during the past decade, for Dave has served in Spain for eighteen months and has been overseas for years. She talks of what she and Dave will do when he comes home. They will, she says, move to the country. There are some sharp and eloquent scenes in which the members of the family talk of their hopes and dreams for the future. Life has been hard, but illusions die hard, too. Then Harry has his first stroke, and, even though he has not been the strong-minded member of the Kahn family, the life of the group changes now that Harry is truly ill.

Sarah dreams of Ronnie's being a writer. Harry has a deep sense of failure—and so the years pass. In 1955 Harry has another stroke, and now he is so paralyzed that he can no longer work. Only in his fifties, he is a wreck of a man. There are fleeting references to Ronnie's search to find himself, to Ada's and Dave's experiment in socialist living in Norfolk. Relatives enter and leave, talking about socialism, Communism, and the old days of the East End. Life is a formidable foe. The Soviet Union, in 1956, crushes the Hungarian revolution. Ronnie taunts his mother, and again political talk flares up. Sarah remains a believer, while Ronnie is a realist and Ada has fled London. Harry is senile and doesn't count.

III   *Wesker's Ideology*

Chicken Soup with Barley is not so dramatic as *Roots*, but it has more set speeches than either *Roots* or *I'm Talking About Jerusalem*. It was written by a playwright who may not have known, at the time of writing, that he would extend the lives of the Kahn family across three plays, and so he packed into *Chicken Soup with Barley* most of his social and political ideas. He also lingered longer over his characters here than he did in the other plays. It is a solid work and very important as a guide to Wesker's thinking.[7]

Sarah, in the midst of a family quarrel, discusses socialism with relatives and friends and complains that cold and calculating people can't teach love and brotherhood. She is advised that "love comes later," but Sarah refuses to believe this. "You have to start with love," she insists. "How can you talk about socialism otherwise?"

Ada has accepted her mother's view of the world, but has her own variation to offer. She explains why she and Dave will leave London, and why she will live her own kind of socialism. Her mother, in *I'm Talking About Jerusalem,* does not understand Ada's motivation, although it is clearly stated in *Chicken Soup with Barley:*

When Dave comes back we shall leave London and live in the country. That'll be our socialism. Remember this, Ronnie: the family should be a unit, and your work and your life should be part of one existence, not something hacked about by a bus queue and office hours. A man should see, know, and love his job. Don't you want to feel your life? Savour it gently? In the country we shall be somewhere where the air doesn't smell of bricks and the kids can grow up without seeing grandparents who are continually shouting at each other.

Ronnie argues with her. He charges her with deserting humanity, at a time when the British Labour Party has a majority in the House of Commons and when there are two Communist members in the House.[8] Ronnie sees a new time coming. He visualizes the nationalization of industries, national health plans, new hospitals, schools, and cities. He reminds his sister that Dave has fought in Spain and will not agree to a cessation of political activity. Ada's answer to her brother, who still has his own kind of dreams, is: "I do not believe in the right to organize people." Then she makes an astute statement, which also reflects the utter honesty with which Wesker presents many sides of an argument: "And anyway I'm not so sure that I love them enough to *want* to organize them."

Sarah is saddened to hear this, for her daughter had been a dedicated organizer. But now Ada has other ideas. She is beginning to think of herself and her husband as individuals:

I'm tired, mother. I spent eighteen months waiting for Dave to return from Spain and now I've waited six years for him to come home from a war against Fascism and I'm tired. Six years in and out of offices, auditing books and working with young girls who are morons—lipsticked, giggling morons. And Dave's experience is the same—fighting with men who he says did not know what the war was about. Away from their wives they behaved like animals. In fact they wanted to get away from their wives in order to behave like animals. Give them another war and they'd run back again. Oh yes! the service killed any illusions Dave may have once had about the splendid and heroic working class.[9]

[38]

Harry claims that the Communist Party wants to do away with the jungle that society has become. Sarah says that life must and does carry on, that a man "still has children, he laughs, he finds things to make him laugh." But Ada remains the realist. "You do not want to do away with the jungle," she observes. "You have *never* cried against the jungle of an industrial society. You've never wanted to destroy its *values*—simply to own them yourselves."

The following year Dave and Ada are in the Fens in Norfolk, trying to live the life dreamed of by Ada. Harry has suffered from his stroke for fourteen months now and is "like an autumn leaf" in a strong wind. He has realized his own failure as a man and as a father. As for Dave and Ada, they are, in Ronnie's words, "struggling in a tied cottage in the country. Ada suckles a beautiful baby, Dave lays concrete floors in the day-time and makes furniture by hand in the evening. . . . They're happy. Two Jews in the Fens! They had to get a Rabbi from Norwich to circumcise the baby. A Rabbi from Norwich! Who'd ever think there were Rabbis in Norwich!" [10]

While Ada and Dave seek fulfillment in the country and Sarah retains her dreams of Communism, Harry continues to decline in health and his weakness becomes more and more apparent to his son, Ronnie: "Your weakness frightens me, Harry. . . . I watch you and I see myself and I'm terrified." Harry is a realist, a sad one. "What I am—I am," he informs his son. "I will never alter. I'm an old man and if I've been the same all my life so I will always be. You can't alter people, Ronnie. You can only give them some love and hope they'll take it."

Ronnie, who is not an old and beaten man, refuses to listen to his father's advice. But in time he learns that there is something in what Harry has said. The world can easily defeat one, he concludes. He has worked in a kitchen in Paris and hated it. This hatred is not so obvious in the play *The Kitchen*. [11] In it, the people are trapped, perhaps, but Wesker is still groping there and hoping as well. Ronnie, having seen the men and women sweat in the Paris kitchen, concludes that "this notion of earning an honest penny is all my eye." What are we? "People terrified of old age, hoping for the football pools to come home."

Moreover, Ronnie is shocked by what the Soviets did in Hungary. He accuses his mother of blindness, political blindness. What has happened to their dreams? Ronnie cries out to Sarah, "Why do I feel ashamed to use words like democracy and freedom and brotherhood? They don't have meaning any more." He tells his mother that he has lost his faith and his ambition. The family has fallen apart, and Sarah won't face it. "You're a pathological case, Mother—do you know that? You're still a *Communist!*"

Sarah, a fighter, is unwilling to yield to her son. She answers that when there was a depression, and unemployment, everyone was a Communist. Now life is easier; people want money in the bank and television sets. They no longer want to think. "Is that what you want me to be satisfied with—a television set?" Just as Beatie Bryant in *Roots* attains a high degree of eloquence in the final scene of that play, Sarah Kahn now makes her speech: "All my life I worked with a party that meant glory and freedom and brotherhood? You want me to give it up now? . . . I should cut off my light? Socialism is my light, can you understand that? A way of life. A man *can* be beautiful. I hate ugly people—I can't bear meanness and fighting and jealousy—I've got to have light. I'm a simple person, Ronnie, and I've got to have light and love."

She defends herself against Ronnie's silent accusation that she has not properly loved Harry, her husband and Ronnie's father. He, she cries out, never cared: "All I did was fight him because he didn't care. He doesn't care to live. He's never cared to fully undress himself and put on pyjamas; never cared to keep shaved or washed; or be on time or even turn up! . . . He doesn't care! And so I fought him because he didn't care. I fought everybody who didn't care."

There will always be human beings, Sarah says, and as long as human beings exist, we will have the idea of brotherhood. Ronnie claims that brotherhood has no meaning, even though there are human beings. Again, Sarah fights him and tries to make him care, as she failed to make Harry care. If Ronnie has no interest in people, there is nothing. "It all comes down to nothing!" She warns her son that despair can kill: "Despair—die then! Will that be achievement? To die? . . . Please, Ronnie, don't let me finish this life thinking I lived for nothing. We got through, didn't we? We got scars but we got through. You hear me, Ronnie? You've got to care, you've got to care or you'll die." And as the play ends Sarah keeps repeating the words: "You'll die, you'll die—if you don't care you'll die."

Wesker cares. He cares for his people, for his ideas, for the men who have had dreams and seen them crushed by life. Sarah fights to the end. Harry doesn't. Ada tries. Ronnie cannot make up his mind. We see what happens to Ronnie in *Roots*, and we trace the William Morris experiment in *I'm Talking About Jerusalem*. Wesker has set the stage for the Kahns in *Chicken Soup with Barley*, but he has done more than that. He also has awakened the British working people, at least those who hear his voice. Unlike the early John Osborne, who has concentrated on individuals and their personal problems—their sexual conflicts, their love affairs—Wesker has wrestled with politics and ideas. He does this in all of his plays, and not least in the first drama in the Wesker Trilogy.

CHAPTER 4

Roots

R OOTS, the middle play of the Wesker Trilogy, is the most powerful and eloquent of the three dramas; it most clearly expresses Wesker's sense of dismay over the indifference of the working class toward improving itself and finding its own voice. Bernard Levin in his Introduction to the Penguin edition of *Roots* points out that

the villain in *Roots* is the society that treads these people into the dirt and then affects to despise them when some of it gets onto their clothes and won't brush off. It is, of course, a fiercely political play, despite its very overtly political references; Mr. Wesker, I take it, is a Socialist, not because he thinks working-class people are the best in the land, but because he does not. The play, after all, is called *Roots,* and not because that was the first word that came into Mr. Wesker's head. If the roots are poisoned, the plant will not flower; if the plant flowers, there must be healthy roots below.[1]

I *Apathy and Thoughtlessness*

Roots is set in Norfolk and deals with country people living at some distance from London. Beatie Bryant (brilliantly inter-preted by Joan Plowright in the London version of the play first presented in 1959) is a young woman in love with Ronnie Kahn, a Londoner who never appears on stage in this drama; Ronnie's presence is strongly felt, however, because Beatie is constantly quoting him. Beatie returns from London to her family in Norfolk and awaits the appearance of Ronnie, whom she plans to intro-duce to the clan before they marry. Ronnie is an intellectual, an idealist who tries to stir Beatie and force her to think. Her family, unlettered and inarticulate, is content to live in dirt and squalor and is unwilling to think through the consequences of the empti-ness of its life. Beatie harangues them, talks to them incessantly of

Ronnie and of his cultural and social ideas and ideals. She cannot make an impact on their minds, and Wesker shows through their actions and seeming apathy, how difficult it is to awaken the farm laborer to the wider world, to classical books, to great music, to politics.

Beatie, upon her return to Norfolk, comes to the home of her sister and brother-in-law, Jenny and Jimmy Beales. Jenny is "short, fat, and friendly," and Jimmy is a garage mechanic. From the beginning, Beatie attempts to convince Jenny and Jimmy of the importance of her Ronnie. They remain unconvinced. Jimmy, annoyed, says to her: "Beatie—you bin away from us a long time now—you got a boy who's educated an' that and he's taught you a lot maybe. But don't you come pushin' ideas across at us—we're alright as we are."

In truth, Beatie isn't quite convinced herself about Ronnie's ideas. She loves him; she wishes to marry him and to have his babies. Romantically, she feels that after marriage intellectual and idealistic talk will be less important than having a family. She had been a waitress in the hotel where Ronnie worked in the kitchen.[2] She fell in love with him, chased him, made love with him, and heeded his words; but she was far more interested in Ronnie than in what he said.

Beatie confides in Jenny: "He was interested in all the things I never even thought about. About politics and art and all that, and he tried to teach me. He's a socialist and he used to say you couldn't bring socialism by making speeches, but perhaps you could pass it on to someone who was near you. So I pretended I was interested—but I didn't understand much. All the time he's trying to teach me but I can't take it, Jenny. And yet, at the same time, I want to show I'm willing. I'm not used to learning. Learning was at school and that's finished with."

When Beatie visits her mother's home, she again has trouble conveying the significance of Ronnie's ideas. Beatie is eager for her parents to be "decent" when Ronnie comes. But the conflict, the real clash of views and the puzzlement in her mind, is that she is not quite sure what "decent" means to Ronnie. Beatie does not understand Ronnie and so she asks her parents not to swear, not to be "dirty," although she confesses that Ronnie swears. "Yes," she admits, "but I don't want him to hear *you* swear." Somewhat pathetically, she says, "I don't want Ronnie to think I come from a small-minded family."

Beatie's parents listen stolidly to her constant chatter. Her mother gossips about the neighbors and her father talks of his health. Mrs. Bryant is indifferent to Beatie's exhortations about culture. When Beatie hears how her mother listens to popular songs, she asks: "How do the words affect you? Are you moved? Do you find them beautiful?" "Them's as good words as any," Mrs. Bryant replies. "But do they make you feel better?" Beatie persists. Mrs. Bryant is annoyed. "Blust gal! Them ent supposed to be a laxative!"

Beatie argues that her mother's taste is for third-rate material. Mrs. Bryant does not worry about ratings; she likes what she likes, and Beatie, in all honesty, is on her mother's side. One of Ronnie's irritations is that Beatie has acted like her own mother and that she has interpreted and reduced his ideas into lower-middle-class clichés. "I'm worried about Ronnie," Beatie confides to her mother. "I have the same row with him. I ask him exactly the same questions—what make a pop song third-rate. And he answers and I don't know what he talk about." Ronnie had advised her to "talk and look and listen and think and ask questions." Plaintively, Beatie cries: "But Jesus! I don't know what questions to ask or *how* to talk."

In the end, Ronnie sends a letter to Beatie, informing her that he will not come to Norfolk, that he will not marry her, because, he admits, his ideas are "useless and romantic." The family taunts Beatie, who is seeking certain satisfactions in life which she senses are valuable but does not quite understand herself.

The play ends in a burst of eloquence and its conclusion is only the beginning for Beatie, who realizes that she has been mouthing the thoughts of Ronnie and has been doing no thinking of her own. Beatie dominates the stage in this final scene and her speech remains Arnold Wesker's finest achievement and clearest statement of his own philosophy and social outlook.

Meanwhile, Wesker has touched lightly but sharply on other issues. An old man, Stan Mann, lusty as an old goat, remembers his sexual prowess and more: he looks at the world that is alive. Then, suddenly, he dies. Mrs. Bryant gossips about one Jimmy Skelton: "They say he've bin arrested for accosting some man in the village." But Mrs. Bryant is generous enough not to condemn him. And Mr. Bryant tries desperately to hide from the manager of the farm where he is employed the true condition of his health.

II *Survival But No Communication*

The spectator and the reader are also introduced to the silent, almost mute, laborers who mistrust the world and even themselves. One notes with some surprise that Beatie's father does not allow her to bake a cake because he refuses to pay the electric bill, although the cake is intended for Beatie's sister and Mr. Bryant's own daughter. Yet he eagerly helps Beatie prepare her bath. The characters are full of paradoxes, for they are both mean and generous, indifferent and friendly. Clearly, they have potential, and their dullness is only a cover. But they have never realized their potential, which is why Wesker is angry with them—and with the society that produced them. In his interviews, in his articles, and in some of his nondramatic writings, Wesker has continued to point out that he *likes* his almost inarticulate farmers, that they are the victims less of themselves than of their society. And when critics call his people "dull," Wesker is upset. He feels that they have a generous nature, that they have wit, and, most important, that they have the ability to survive.

As Wesker's narration develops, the reader becomes aware (as does the spectator), that this is a play of ideas as well as atmosphere. It is after the Bryant family has been gathered together to await the coming of Ronnie—and when Ronnie's letter arrives—that the play takes fire. Up to this moment Wesker has captured the atmosphere of a farm laborer's home; he has drawn, in broad terms, the characteristics of a handful of selected people who are types rather than individuals. The play does not quite dawdle, but it is by no means a fast-moving drama. It does, however, reach a strong climax. Mrs. Bryant reads aloud Ronnie's letter, which is, within the context of the drama, explosive. "My ideas about handing on a new kind of life to people are quite useless and romantic," Ronnie informs Beatie. "If I were a healthy human being," the letter continues, "it might have been alright but most of us intellectuals are pretty sick and neurotic—as you have often observed—and we couldn't build a world even if we were given the reins of government—not yet any rate."

As her family listens to Beatie talk, all of them are puzzled by what she says and why she says it. "I got no roots in nothing," she explains. "I come from a family o' farm laborers yet I ent got no roots—just like town people—just a mass o' nothin'." When her brother Frankie wants to know what she means by roots, Beatie replies: "Root, roots, roots! Christ, Frankie, you're in the fields all day, you should know about growing things. Roots! The things you come from, the things that feed you. The things that make you proud of yourself—roots!"

Beatie is disturbed because she is not reaching her family; she is caustic because her family doesn't care about the problem of the atom bomb; she is indignant that everyone seems bored. Her mother challenges her and asks, how can one be bored with a radio and television? Again, Beatie tells them that radio, television, and the movies are the easy way out: "Anything so long as we don't have to make an effort. Well, am I right? You know I'm right. Education ent only books and music—it's asking questions, all the time. There are millions of us, all over the country and no one, not one of us is asking questions, we're all taking the easiest way out."

At the end of Wesker's final play in this trilogy, *I'm Talking About Jerusalem*, Ronnie's brother-in-law, Dave, remarks to Ronnie that he hadn't the courage to "see a sordid love affair through" meaning, of course, Ronnie's relationship with Beatie. Ronnie here replies, "It wasn't sordid, you know, Dave. I know I didn't see it through to the end but it wasn't sordid. Beatie Bryant could have been a poem—I gave her words—maybe she became one."

Beatie's final passage, which is quoted in part or in whole elsewhere in this study (and in many essays and volumes about British drama), is the "poem" that Ronnie talks about to Dave. Here, within the context of *Roots*, is that often quoted and highly praised passage:

Do you think we really count? You don' wanna take any notice of what them ole papers say about the workers bein' all important these days —that's all squit! 'Cos we aren't. Do you think when the really talented people in the country get to work they get to work for us? Hell if they do! Do you think they don't know we 'ont make the effort? The writers don't write thinkin' we can understand, nor the painters don't paint expecting us to be interested—that they don't, nor don't the composers give out music thinking we can appreciate it. "Blust," they say, "the masses is too stupid for us to come down to them. Blust," they say, "If they don't make no effort why should we bother?" So you know who come along? The slop singers and the pop writers and the film makers and women's magazines and the Sunday papers and the picture strip love stories—that's who come along, and you don't have to make no effort for them, it come easy. "We know where the money lie," they say. "Hell we do! The workers've got it so let's give them what they want. If they want slop songs and film idols we'll give 'em that then. If they want the third rate, BLUST! We'll give 'em THAT then. Anything's good enough for them 'cos they don't ask for no more!" The whole stinkin' commercial world insults us and we don't care a damn. Well, Ronnie's right—it's our own bloody fault. We want the third-rate—we got it! We got it! We. . . .

Suddenly, Beatie realizes that she is now doing her own thinking, "I'm not quoting any more," she announces triumphantly—and her life is now ready to begin. The final scene in *Roots* shook and changed the British stage; it placed Wesker in the forefront of those new dramatists who were writing about the working people, their complaints, their search for something better, their wish to improve themselves. Beatie's awakening, which takes place on stage, which is not talked about but is demonstrated through the use of powerful and eloquent words, is an awakening for an entire segment of the British population.

It is no wonder, then, that the reader of this play turns back to Wesker's brief but important note to *Roots*, the Note to Actors and Producers in which he states: "My people are not caricatures, they are real (though fiction). And though the picture I have drawn of them is a harsh one, yet still my tone is not of disgust—nor should it be in the presentation of this play. I am at one with these people—it is only that I am annoyed with them and myself."

III *The Impact of Roots*

Roots was of the utmost importance to Wesker for a variety of reasons. It was, of course, a critical success, but it was something more than that: it made many Englishmen aware of his gifts and led to the staging of his earlier as well as his later dramas. John

Dexter has written: "I did not begin to catch the real flavour of Arnold's writing until *Roots*. . . . *Roots* opened the way to *The Kitchen* and the production of the *Trilogy* and all the experiments, good and bad, which sprang from them." [4]

It should be pointed out that *Roots,* when it was exported to the United States, made very little impact on American audiences, although the New York newspaper critics dutifully reviewed it, in spite of the fact that it was an off-Broadway production.[5] By the time *Roots* was brought to the United States, Wesker's name had begun to have some slight familiarity to American theater-lovers —mainly to those who, on a trip to London, make it their business to enjoy the British stage.

Robert Hatch has intelligently analyzed the impression made by *Roots* in this country—and the reasons for it. In *Horizon* he writes: "The whole trilogy should be brought here. *Roots* by itself distorts Wesker's ideas by making them seem more naïve than they are. Without the other plays, moreover, Ronnie looks like a villain, and that compromises the author's purpose. Ronnie is a latter-day everyman, faulty, confused, driven by the genius of self-dissatisfaction. He is a considerable creation: in his own Jewish way, the sort of man the Irish put on their stage." [6]

In discussing the New York production of *Roots,* Hatch also explains its failure:

Roots was not very well produced in New York; it is a difficult play to stage with American personnel. The kind of country worker Wesker describes does not exist here, and though our culture may be debased, it is not stagnant. Cut off from our roots, we racket all over the place; Wesker's people are withering, like marrows with their roots severed beneath them. The cast seemed to be visiting the play, not living in it; and the production, lacking a security of location and tone, fell off into staginess. Further, the young actress who played Beatie displayed the wrong kind of vitality. She suggested a sociology major on a rampage, and since much of what she mouthed was platitudinous, she sounded more stupid than ignorant. Wesker does not waste pity on stupidity; he is the champion of the uninformed. But despite a fallible production, and although I have reservations about the Wesker gospel, *Roots* goes on ringing in my ears as few plays have recently.[7]

Other American critics had their own reservations, and *Roots* came and went quietly.

IV *British Critical Response*

The English critics, however, were far more moved and stirred by *Roots*. While practically all of them recognized the play as good theater and realized that in Wesker a new star had risen, they argued more about it from the point of view of its message.

Anthony Hartley sets *Roots* within an intellectual and sociological context. He is unhappy about Wesker's attack on the society in which Hartley himself is most comfortable. "Culturally," Hartley has written in *A State of England,* "England is being divided into intellectuals and the rest. What we are seeing is the equilization of everything below a rather high cultural level, and this process does not reflect class differences in the usual sense, since, though intellectuals generally live like the professional middle classes, they cannot be entirely identified with them." [8]

Having set the stage, Hartley argues with Wesker's concept of the role of the intellectual and claims that *Roots* both exaggerates and diminishes that role. Ronnie, according to Hartley, is not a good intellectual. "Most of the things he is represented as saying here and in the other two plays of Mr. Wesker's trilogy are the commonplaces of a vague populism, which makes up in moral fervour what it lacks in precise objectives." [9] Then Hartley comes to the core of his case: "It is not the primary duty of an intellectual to go round as a kind of cultural missionary bent on converting the heathen. His primary duty is to improve the quality of his thought and, if he is a creative artist, of his works. And if he takes any other view of his task in life he will not have anything worth saying to communicate—this, incidentally, seems to be the case with Ronnie Kahn." [10]

Richard Findlater is indifferent to the strictures of Anthony Hartley. Although he acknowledges that *Roots* moves at too slow a pace, he has called Wesker "a major dramatist in the making, with one play of lasting value already to his credit," that play being *Roots*. Findlater recognizes Wesker's social significance, as well as his dramatic gift:

Socially, his plays are important because they introduce members of
the "working class"—and, in particular, the *rural* working class—as
human beings with rights of their own on the stage, instead of as
comic silhouettes and stereotypes; and this is an innovation no less
significant and valuable because in the last three years the West End
managers have suddenly flooded the market with proles *a la mode.*
Roots may be considered as a milestone in the modern English drama,
on linguistic and sociological grounds alone. What is more important,
however, and it is very hard to define in a few sentences, is Wesker's
attitude towards his characters: a burning moral concern, fuelled by
compassion and forgiveness, blazing up in a flare of theatrical life
force. This author labours to show the love between people, especially
people in a family; to affirm their essential individual value, as members of mankind, and to remind the audience that they belong to it,
too.[11]

Laurence Kitchin, like Findlater and unlike Hartley, has found
Roots to be a remarkable play; he calls it "one of the most enlight-
ening experiences I have ever been given in a theatre." [12] He has
made one strong point by saying, "Instead of luxuriating in out-
worn proletarian gestures of protest, it faces the fact that igno-
rance, not poverty, is the enemy now to be grappled with in Britain." [13]

In one of the most intensive and penetrating critiques on Wesker, John Mander has called *Roots* a major play of our time. He
considers it far superior to Osborne's *Look Back in Anger.*

Roots, Mander asserts, is frequently praised for "its documentary qualities," but he continues: "if the play is no more than a
slice-of-life, then no documentary authenticity will make it a better work of art than *Look Back in Anger,* or *Room at the Top.* Yet
it is, I think, very much superior artistically to either of these." [14]
Why? Mander answers in this fashion:

In the first place, those who praise *Roots* for its Naturalism have, I
think, got hold of the wrong end of the stick. The dialect may be ac-
curately rendered and the observation may be good; but these things
are artistically secondary. Primary, as in any work of art, is the structure; and it is the efficient dialectical structure of *Roots* that puts it in
a wholly different category from *Look Back in Anger.* This underlying
dialectic demands, certainly, the most careful realisation in speech
and action. But *Roots* would still be a considerable achievement even

if it could be shown that Mr. Wesker had exaggerated the number of ailments from which Norfolk peasants suffer, and make a hash of the dialect. The documentary truthfulness is important, then, but secondary. . . .[15]

Mander finds Wesker superior to Auden, Spender, Isherwood, and George Orwell;[16] he adds that "Mr. Wesker's understanding both of the English working class and of Socialism must seem far more mature and more considered than Orwell's." [17] His reason is that "Mr. Wesker's starting position as the child of Jewish immigrants, born within a tradition of Socialist political activity and political thought, was perhaps more favourable than Orwell's as an Eton Colleger. Mr. Wesker had the advantage of being a partial outsider in class-divided English society." [18]

John Russell Taylor considers *Roots* inferior to *Chicken Soup with Barley* and believes that Joan Plowright was principally responsible for its acceptance as a drama of value.[19] Many of the other notices of *Roots* were mixed.

I saw *Roots* in London at the Royal Court Theatre and was struck with fact that the audience was primarily a working-class audience. The so-called slowly paced scenes were observed closely and appreciatively. The set speeches were cheered wildly. Joan Plowright, who played difficult scenes with aplomb, carried off the role brilliantly. But, although I was an American sitting among Englishmen, I could not but be moved by what was said as well as by how it was stated. I felt that perhaps *Roots* was too specialized for American audiences, that the "social protest" play had reached its peak in the United States decades earlier and that *Roots* might appear to be "old-fashioned" to Americans, whether or not Joan Plowright was its star. There is little doubt that it moved English spectators and made the stage meaningful as well as dramatic to them.

CHAPTER 5

I'm Talking About Jerusalem

I'M *Talking About Jerusalem,* which rounds out the Wesker Trilogy, is, quite on its own, a drama of exciting and original ideas.
The "Jerusalem" of the title is not the Jerusalem in Israel but the
new Jerusalem of William Morris, who believed in the idealism of
socialism. Clearly, too, the title was drawn from William Blake's
lines: "Till we have built Jerusalem/ In England's green and pleasant land." The individuals who were introduced in *Chicken Soup
with Barley* and *Roots* are by now familiar to us and we are interested to know what has happened to them, even if schemes, love
affairs, and dreams end in failure and frustration. Wesker, quite
obviously, has created a family, and midway through *I'm Talking
About Jerusalem,* a play taut with ideas, we discover how Ronnie
Kahn feels about Beatie Bryant; how Ronnie fits in with his sister
Ada; and how Ada and her husband Dave Simmonds seek a new
Jerusalem, but find that their dream is doomed to failure.

I *The Story Based on Fact*

I'm Talking About Jerusalem is the story of Ada and Dave, who
reject London and attempt to lead a life close to the earth in Norfolk, where Dave is a carpenter and Ada a housewife. Theirs is a
Utopian dream. What happens to it is the story of the play.

It seems like a simple story, yet some English critics have wondered whether it has a realistic base. John Russell Taylor is caustic
when he describes the play as one in which a couple leave for the
country "to live a life of Morrisian devotion to arts and crafts,
to individual toil in which a man can be his own master away
from the domination of the industrialist and the machine. The
idea of a pair of Jewish intellectuals doing this in 1946 is clearly
unusual, even improbable, enough to suggest that this time the

[52]

author's intention cannot possibly be a simple reflection of life as it is normally lived—the very title implies a parable. And so, surely, the play must be judged." [1]

Taylor is wrong if he believes that *I'm Talking About Jerusalem* is a parable, an imaginative account of two dreamers conceived in the mind of the playwright. *I'm Talking About Jerusalem* is dedicated to "Della and Ralph." Della is Arnold Wesker's sister, and Ralph is Ralph Saltiel, his brother-in-law. Ralph Saltiel and I met when we were both in the service of our countries during World War II. I was a radio operator in Colombo, Ceylon; Ralph was with the Air Sea Rescue, British boat-building unit in Colombo. Ralph was a brilliant, dynamic, exciting human being who swore that, should he survive the war, he would live as a simple working man, using his hands as a carpenter. He was a socialist, a Jew, and a man with a strong sense of justice and idealism.

Apparently, Arnold Wesker was deeply impressed by his brother-in-law, and *I'm Talking About Jerusalem* is based on Ralph's and Della's experiences over a ten-year period spent living, experimentally as it were, in a humble shack in Norfolk. In the play, Ada and Dave manage to exist in Norfolk from 1946 to 1959, a longer time than the ten years spent by Ralph and Della in Norfolk. The essential facts, however, are as the real-life couple lived them.

When I visited Ralph Saltiel in London in 1960, he was as exciting a person as I had remembered him, but he no longer was a struggling carpenter in the British countryside. He sported a trim and artistic Van Dyke and was a successful interior decorator who was busily furnishing the homes of wealthy British playwrights and businessmen. His wife, who resembles her brother, was chic and quiet and the devoted mother of two sons. Visiting with them, one could hardly imagine that they had lived for so long a time under such difficult circumstances; but they had.

Wesker makes this very clear in the first act. Dave tells his mother-in-law, Sarah Kahn (the strong character of *Chicken Soup with Barley*), why he and Ada have decided to leave London. Sarah says, "The city is human beings. What's socialism without human beings—tell me?"

Dave replies:

I know the city, Sarah. Believe me, sweetheart! Since being demobbed
I've worked in a factory turning out doors and window frames and
I've seen men hate themselves while they were doing it. Morning
after morning they've come in with a cold hatred in their eyes, brutal-
ized! All their humanity gone. These you call men! All their life they're
going to drain their energy into something that will give them nothing
in return . . . Ten yards from me, where I can see and hear them,
will be my family. And they will share in my work and I shall share
in their lives. I don't want to be married to strangers. I've seen the city
make strangers of husbands and wives, but not me, not me and my
wife.

Dave makes his defiance clear, although his mother-in-law and
Ronnie, his brother-in-law, don't understand him. Ronnie, at one
point, says, "The wandering Jews strike again! None of the easy
life for them, none of the comforts of electricity. . . ."
Dave (like Ralph) had been inspired to make his move when
he saw people working in Ceylon (again evidence that this is not
Taylor's parable but fact):

Being a carpenter I used to watch the local carpenters at work. They
used to make their own tools and sometimes they'd show me. They'd
sit out on the beach fashioning the boats or outside their houses plan-
ing and chiselling away at their timber and they let me sit with them
once they knew I was also building boats. And you know, one day,
as I watched, I made a discovery—the kind of discovery you discover
two or three times in a lifetime. I discovered an old truth: that a man
is made to work and that when he works he's giving away something
of himself, something very precious. . . .

Thus Dave explains himself. Sarah listens and sings a melodic
Yiddish folk song. Her son and daughter join her, and finally
Dave also sings with them, as his new life begins. But he is chal-
lenged all along the road. His employer scarcely talks to him.
Dave and Ada realize that people think of them as "rustics, escap-
ists, soft-headed." Dave's army friend, Libby Dobson, who comes
to visit them, taunts Dave for his idealism and challenges him on
his move to the country. Dobson says, "Be heroic! There's nothing
wrong with idealism, only when it's soft and flabby. The smell of
petrol in my nose! So what! You can't change the world because it
smells of petrol." Dobson continues his challenge: "Have you ever

taken your ideas to their logical conclusion? Well, have you? Hasn't a worker in a factory ever looked at you as though you were mad—a little potty, you know? Will you have the world do without cars, planes, electricity, houses, roads? Because that's the logical conclusion. . . ." Dave has his own response: "Do you think we care that the city was large or smelt of petrol? It was the boredom, man—the sheer boredom. Nine to five! Mass production! Remember? It numbed us, made us soggy and soft."

But Dobson is now a cynic, and it is indicative of Wesker's fairness to offer both sides through his spokesmen. Dobson insists that he had tried socialism and it had failed. He is now a businessman. He rejects democracy and praises "benevolent dictatorship." He declares, "You want Jerusalem. Order it with an iron hand—no questions, no speeches for and against—bang! It's there! You don't understand it? You don't want it? Tough luck, comrade—your children will."

What this play is really about is a man's effort to escape the grind of our mechanized economy, our teeming cities, our hunt for wealth and status. In the end, Dave and Ada fail to make a success of their experiment. Dave's employer fires him when Dave takes, without permission, a bit of linoleum. He begins to make his own furniture and takes special joy in creating something with his own hands. He is not "messing around." He is "creating," as he puts it, "for the sheer enjoyment."

Dave and Ada work without the encouragement of their family. They raise a family of their own; they work hard; they struggle; but they get no sympathy. From time to time, Kahn family members visit them, argue with them, make fun of them. Dave hears them out and finally explodes: "Ten years I spent here trying to carve out a satisfactory life for my wife and kids and on every side we've had opposition. From the cynics, the locals, the family. Everyone was choking with their experience of life and wanted to hand it on. Who came forward with a word of encouragement? Who said we maybe had a little guts? Who offered one tiny word of praise?"

The Simmondses give up. Dave and Ronnie talk about their generation and what they have been trying to do. Dave reflects on World War II and remarks, "A useless, bloody war because Hitler still made it, didn't he, eh? And out went six million Jews in little puffs of smoke." Then Dave tells Ronnie, bitterly, about his dreams:

What do you think I am, Ronnie? You think I'm an artist's craftsman? Nothing of that sort. A designer? Not even that. Designers are ten a penny . . . I've reached the point where I can face the fact that I'm not a prophet. Once I had—I don't know—a—moment of vision and I yelled at your Aunty Esther that I was a prophet . . . we came here, we worked hard, we've loved every minute of it and we're still young. Do you expect anything else? You wanted us to grow to be giants, didn't you? The mighty artist craftsman! Well, now the only things that seem to matter to me are the day-to-day problems of my wife, my kids and my work. Face it—as an essential member of society I don't really count.

To Wesker, Dave and Ada represent all who sometimes feel they must rebel against the world as it is. One may not succeed; one may fail; but one must continue to try.

II *Verbal Passion*

In his Introduction to *I'm Talking About Jerusalem* Robert Muller pays tribute to Wesker's passion when he writes, "This kind of verbal ardour is rare on the English stage . . . One has to go back to Strindberg and Toller to discover a parallel faith in personal experience as the raw material for didactic dramaturgy." [2] He adds that Wesker has "the honesty of innocence" to put the blame for Dave's and Ada's failure on their own weaknesses as well as on a hostile society. "It is this innocence," Muller informs us, "rather than his political fervour, which helps us to find the key to Wesker's work up to now; the innocence that permits a gift for primitive lyricism full reign, the innocence that allows him to mine his plays out of the seam of personal experience without recourse to the brake of inhibition." [3]

James Gindin comes to the same conclusion reached by Muller, when he writes that *I'm Talking About Jerusalem* "does not depict the failure of a social ideal. Rather, the play presents the failure of two individuals, of Ada and her husband, to shape their lives in terms of the William Morris kind of ideal." [4]

It is John Russell Taylor who has recognized a problem faced by Wesker when, in *I'm Talking About Jerusalem*, he attempted to "throw over naturalism and even realism altogether in favour of a far more adaptable and adventurous means of dramatic expression." [5] John Dexter the director, has said that *I'm Talking About Jerusalem* "was for me a long farewell to naturalism, atmosphere and illusion." [6]

So it is evident that Wesker has taken facts from real life and made a poetic drama out of them. Based on realism, *I'm Talking About Jerusalem* has "taken off," and become a cry for a change in the mechanized life of the city man. The new form adapted by Wesker in *Chips with Everything* becomes more understandable if we recognize that *I'm Talking About Jerusalem*, the final play of the Wesker Trilogy, is both the ending of one cycle and the artistic beginning of another.

CHAPTER 6

Chips with Everything

THE dramatic talents of Arnold Wesker were not apparent to American theater-goers until *Chips with Everything* reached Broadway on October 1, 1963. The drama had a fairly good run of four months (closing on February 8, 1964, after 149 performances), but, more importantly, it made a strong critical impact, and suddenly New York newspapers, national magazines, and various television programs featured Wesker both as a playwright and as the leader of the Centre 42 movement. *The Kitchen*, as a film, was seen by few Americans. The three plays about the Kahns were—and are—not yet known to American audiences. Wesker is known as the author of *Chips with Everything* in the United States.

This is not surprising, for it was *Chips with Everything* that brought Wesker his first West End success in London. Indeed, *Chips with Everything* has become an international success. In England it disturbed the Establishment; in the United States it interested audiences. Harold Hobson, reviewing the play in London's Sunday *Times*, said, "This is the Left-wing drama's first real breakthrough, the first anti-Establishment play of which the Establishment has cause to be afraid. If there is a better play in London I haven't seen it. This is something to be discussed and rediscussed, admired, feared." [1]

Wesker is aiming mainly at the British Establishment, and so the critical reviews and reactions in the United States were not so personal as those that were published in England. *Chips with Everything* deals with one of Britain's military services, apparently a brave theme for an Englishman to approach. Americans may be able to analyze *Chips with Everything* more calmly, if less subjectively.

Chips with Everything

I *Form and Story*

Chips with Everything is a play in two acts with a total of twenty-three scenes, eleven in the first act and twelve in the second. Wesker's text is short; he offers his scenes in impressionistic, journalistic, almost documentary styles. Some of the finest theatrical scenes in the play take only a half page or a page of stage direction in the written version, or depend more on the action than on the spoken word. The staging is almost all-important. John Dexter, in the New York version (and I assume the London version as well), directed the drama with imagination and staged it almost poetically. While some of the scenes read well, the entire play performs brilliantly. Less talky than the Trilogy, *Chips with Everything* has the incessant movement of *The Kitchen*, but it is far more dramatic, sharper, more individualized.

Chips with Everything is the story of Pip Thompson, the son of a former British general, who has been drafted into the Royal Air Force. It is Pip's story and that of eight other conscripts, who are being molded into conforming soldiers, or airmen. The air force leadership has contempt for all the conscripts, except for Pip, who comes from a higher class. Pip wants to be "one of the boys." The leadership cadre considers him a traitor to his class. As Pip demonstrates qualities of leadership among the conscripts, he is also fighting against those who want him to take his proper place—above the ranks. Pip works hard for acceptance among the airmen, who do not trust him because he is not truly one of their own. In the end, he yields. He finds he cannot live in the world for which he was not prepared and which mistrusts him. He hates his own class, but is of it. He cannot excape his destiny. He cannot leave the Establishment.

II *Chilling and Vivid*

Yet *Chips with Everything* is by no means about the struggle of one man. It is a chilling depiction of military life, and it portrays the officers, the conscripts, and the Royal Air Force with theatrical vividness. In the very first scene we meet Corporal Hill, whose job it is to transform a group of young civilians into soldiers. The sequences in which he harangues his men, stresses their responsibilities, puts them through interminable drills, orders them to take good care of their rifles, and urges them to complete their bayonet drill are all convincing and come alive.

Yet Corporal Hill himself, like the men he is training, is a victim of the system. He introduces himself to his charges by saying, "My name is Corporal Hill. I'm not a very happy man. I don't know why. I never smile and I never joke—you'll soon see that. Perhaps it's my nature, perhaps it's the way I've been brought up—I don't know. The R.A.F. brought me up." Hill warns his men to play fair with him. He urges them to "do me proud." He mothers them and drives them. He is the professional soldier, from the "lower classes." We always remember this fact.

Pip Thompson, whose father is now a banker, was born in a large country house. He is rich and he hates his father. His mates realize he is different from them. One of them, Smiler (who isn't really smiling but whose face is set in a permanent smile), accuses Pip of being a snob, while Charles, a working-class boy, mistrusts him.

Pip recalls an experience he has had. Once his car broke down, and he found himself walking through the East End. He had been dismayed by the shabbiness of the area and the people. He had gone into a cafe and ordered a cup of tea. The cup was cracked. The cake he was given had no taste. The waitress had cleaned the table with a dirty rag, and the walls were peeling. And the menu, stained with tea, said, "Chips with everything." Reminded of that, Pip mutters, "Chips with every damn thing. You breed babies and you eat chips with everything." This is Pip Thompson's complaint against the unfeeling, unheeding, indifferent working class. He echoes Beatie Bryant in *Roots*, who complains (in Ronnie Kahn's philosophy) about the mediocrity of the working class. And, like so many of Wesker's heroes, Pip wants to change matters.

Before Wesker returns to his theme, he offers a brilliantly conceived scene in which Corporal Hill drills the recruits. He taunts them and warns them and insults them. He drives and commands them, crushes them into conformity. At first the men stand on stage as uncertain, insecure individuals. Before Corporal Hill is finished with them they are marching about sharply and professionally. The observer realizes that the attempt to change these men need not be verbal. It is primarily physical. "We're going to be the happiest family in Christendom, and we're going to move together, as one, as one solitary man," Corporal Hill cries. And in the end he has them moving as one man. There is no individuality. Each man has been pressed into a pattern.

The pattern must also be imposed on their minds. In a caustic, ironic scene, Wesker shows how the conscripts sit in a lecture hall and are forced to listen to the Wing Commander, the Squadron Leader, the Pilot Officer, and the Physical Training Instructor. The Wing Commander tells the men they must be prepared. Prepared for what? He isn't sure himself. "Already the aggressors have a force far superior to ours," but he doesn't say who the "aggressors" are, nor does he care. He has a job to do and he will do it, whether or not he has to think about war and its meaning.

The Squadron Leader speaks to them for not more than a minute or two. It is his task, he informs them, to "ensure respect for authority." He points out to them: "You are here to learn discipline. Discipline is necessary if we are to train you to the maximum state of efficiency, discipline and obedience." He, too, does not question his role and when he invites questions, he does not wait for a response. He says, "Any questions? Thank you," and leaves the lecture hall.

The Pilot Officer, effeminate, fastidious, and articulate, represents a section of the power structure hated by Wesker; the words the playwright puts into his mouth are not, of course, realistic, but they make their point effectively, if exaggeratedly:

All I shall require is cleanliness. It's not that I want rigid men, I want clean men. It so happens, however, that you cannot have clean men without rigid men, and cleanliness requires smartness and ceremony . . . your huts must be spick and span without a trace of dust, because dust carries germs, and germs are unclean. I want a man clean from toe nail to hair root. I want him so clean that he looks unreal. In fact I don't want real men, real men are dirty and nasty, they pick their noses—and scratch their skin, I want unreal, super-real men.

The Physical Training Instructor demands fitness. He wants bodies that are "awake and ringing." He, too, explains what he requires and, like the Pilot Officer, exaggerates: "I hate thin men and detest fat ones. I want you like Greek Gods. You heard of the Greeks? You ignorant troupe of anaemics, you were brought up on tinned beans and television sets, weren't you? You haven't had

ARNOLD WESKER

any exercise since you played knock-a-down-ginger, have you?
Greek Gods, you hear me?"

Following this, in a scene far more effective on stage than in the
script, the Pilot Officer visits the hut and talks with Andrew Mc-
Clore, the hut orderly. It is a sensitive passage, in which the officer
remembers his father, who played the piano well, and in which
the officer makes a tentative move to seduce Andrew, who rejects
him. Finally, the Pilot Officer reveals himself and warns Andrew
not to trust him. "Don't ever trust me to be your friend . . . I
warn you not to be fooled by good nature, we slum for our own
convenience."

Pip Thompson, too, is slumming, according to his mates. The
boys talk of their past, of their future, of their hopes. Corporal
Hill admits that he is not serving in the Royal Air Force because
of the upper classes or "royalty." He's serving for "the people back
'ome." Andrew insists that the Pilot Officer was frightened. And
Charles, representing the working class, loves to listen to Pip talking history, implying that history is on the side of the revolutionaries, not that of royalty. As he speaks, he begins to win over the
conscripts, Charles in particular; even Corporal Hill becomes mel-
low.

III   Class Betrayals

It is during a Christmas Eve party that Pip is confronted by the
officers who feel he is betraying them. The Wing Commander
hates civilians, because all they know is "how to make money,
how to chase girls and kill old women. . . . They have muddled
lives and no purpose in those lives." When the airmen celebrate
Christmas Eve by drinking, talking, and squabbling, the officers
look on contemptuously. "Look at them," the Wing Commander
sneers. "What are they? The good old working class of England.
Am I supposed to bless them all the time for being the salt of the
earth?"

Charles overhears the officers taunting them, and he asks Pip
what is going on. Pip commences to arouse the men about him.
Andrew still doesn't trust him. He feels that Pip is one of "them,"
and never can be one of the members of the working class. He is
part of the Establishment, according to Andrew, and that's that:
"I've known a lot of people like you, Pip. They come drinking in

the pub and talk to us as though we were the salt of the earth, and then, one day, for no reason any of us can see, they go off, drop us as though that was another game they was tired of. I'd give a pension to know why we attract you."

Before Pip can reply to this attack, the Wing Commander invites the conscripts to enjoy themselves—on their own "lower" level. He asks the men to perform, to do "a dirty recitation, or a pop song." He condescends to them, laughs at them, but they surprise him, for Andrew proceeds to recite a religious poem by Robert Burns. The Wing Commander urges them to do something else, "something more cheerful," an Elvis Presley song; in a word, something more "fitting" for an inferior man. Pip sees what the officer is attempting to accomplish. He intervenes and persuades one of the conscripts to sing an old peasant revolt song, "The Cutty Wren."

It is effective theater; rebellion projects itself on the stage. The working-class men have shown themselves capable of flaring up. But they have been led by a superior man, and the Wing Commander recognizes this. He calls Pip to his side and asks, "Why are you fighting me, Thompson? We come from the same side, don't we?" The Wing Commander doesn't understand Pip. "Listen, lad," he tells Pip, "if you've got a fight on with your father that's all right by me, we all fight our fathers, and when we fight them we also fight what they stand for." But he asks for a truce and invites Pip to become one of "them."

Pip and Charles confide in each other. Here, the man of the Establishment is trying to win the favor of the representative of "the people." If he were more educated, Charles says, he might be able to be closer to Pip. But Pip tells him that, so far as Charles is concerned, "it's no good wanting to go to university." They talk and argue, but there is a gulf between them.

Pip demonstrates his qualities of leadership and imagination when he persuades the conscripts to raid the coke yard, which is protected by wire netting and a patrol. The job is carried out with military precision; the result is stunning theater. Pip has been the prime mover in the deed, and Charles, who could not talk with him on the same level, begins to worship Pip because of Pip's efficiency and ability.

Meanwhile, Corporal Hill continues to train the new men. He

shows them how to handle a rifle and warns them that death is a terrible thing. Smiler does badly in the drill and is sent to the guard room, where he is tormented by sadistic guards. The Establishment is beginning to realize that Pip is dangerous and that even men like Smiler may rebel. So Pip is called to meet with the officers, who try to persuade him to become one of them. The Pilot Officer, who had failed to win Andrew, and has shown his own fright, now speaks for the Establishment: "The Air Force is no place to carry on a family war, Pip. This is not a public school, it's a place where old boys grow into young men, believe me." Pip, however, isn't buying this argument. He wishes to be an administration orderly and not an officer. He insults the officers and says he does not enjoy or wish their company.

The Pilot Officer now speaks for all the officers, for the people who run the country, for those who must keep the classes apart: ". . . . we haven't stiffened, we aren't offended, no one is going to charge you or strike you. In fact we haven't really taken any notice. We listen to you, we let other people listen to you but we show no offence. Rather—we applaud you, flatter you for your courage and idealism but—it goes right through us. We listen but we do not hear, we befriend but do not touch you, we applaud but we do not act. To tolerate is to ignore, Thompson." He informs Pip that he will be recommended for officer training because "You will not be a foolish, stiff, Empire-thumping officer—no one believes in those any more. You will be more subtle and you will learn how to deal with all the Pip Thompsons who follow you."

The crisis comes when, during bayonet practice, Pip refuses to attack the dummy, although all the other recruits follow orders. But Pip does not impress the men he wishes to impress. Andrew tells him that his "heroic gestures" will not win gratitude. Again the Establishment goes on the attack. The Pilot Officer makes it clear to Pip. He repeats some of his words, as though in a chant, and then adds new ones, which eventually break down Pip. The Pilot Officer tells him: "We listen but we do not hear, we befriend but do not touch you, we applaud but do not act—to tolerate is to ignore. What did you expect, praise from the boys? Devotion from your mates? Your mates are morons, Thompson, morons. At the slightest hint from us they will disown you . . . You cannot fight us from the outside. Relent boy, at least we understand long sentences."

What does Thompson want? Why does he fight as he does? The Pilot Officer probes Thompson's mind and reveals it, both to Pip Thompson and to the audience: "There's nothing humble about you, is there? Thompson, you wanted to do more than simply share the joy of imparting knowledge to your friends; no, not modesty. Not that. What then? What is not those things, my lad? You and I? Shall I say it? Shall I? Power. Power, isn't it?" Pip could not wield power among his equals, so he sought to impress his power on the "lesser men," among the "good-natured yobs." The Pilot Officer asserts that "no man survives whose motive is discovered." And Pip, after this confrontation, is given another chance to go through the bayonet practice session. This time, he heeds the orders of Corporal Hill. He has capitulated. He had made a tentative gesture at leadership among the working-class men, but he has been beaten by the system.

Charles, who had begun to trust him, who had asked Pip to teach him, to guide him, to lead him, is now thrust aside by the broken Pip. Charles recognizes that Pip has been defeated, and accuses him of having been a slummer, of having fooled him. "You lead and then you run away. . . . You call us mate, but you're a scared old schoolboy."

The rebellion is over. Smiler, who had run away, returns, also broken and defeated. Before our eyes, Pip becomes an officer, stiff, unbending, a bit more understanding, yet not much. "We are not hard men," he informs Charles as the transformation takes place and Pip is now one of the officers, "don't think ill of us, the stories you read, the tales you hear. We are good, honest, hard-working like yourselves. . . ."

Again, the Establishment has conquered.

But has it, really? It is worth pondering, and through the observations of Wesker, his director John Dexter, and the critics, some answers may be forthcoming. Prior to the completion of *Chips with Everything*, Wesker said: "Before I went to Rome, I was working on my new play, *Chips with Everything;* now I have finished the first draft, and in it I do not care about sets and props. I just say that the scene is a serviceman's hut, and it doesn't worry me whether there are beds, or walls, or anything. I am not con-

cerned with scenery. In fact, I am working towards a reduction
not only of scenery, but of dialogue as well." [2]

Of the drama itself, Wesker declared: "I have made large
chunks of it very unnaturalistic—but the bonds with the conven-
tions are so strong that in fact I don't think I could have completely broken away. The Trilogy used conventional construction
and techniques, *but I have always said, right from the beginning,
that if I have any importance at all, it is not because of my style,
but because of what I am saying.*[3] John Dexter, who has worked
closely with Wesker on all of his dramas, has said, "I have not yet
seen a perfect performance of *Chips with Everything*, I do not
suppose I ever shall. The play is elusive." [4] He added, however,
that it is "the most stimulating play I have ever directed." [5]

In the bibliography at the end of this study, I have included a
listing, with essential excerpts, of critical notices and essays on
Wesker's work; the bulk of the comments are on *Chips with
Everything*. I have preferred to offer the listing plus the comments because many of the references come from English journals
which are generally unavailable in this country (particularly back
issues of newspapers). I should, therefore, not wish to repeat
within the body of this chapter all of the comments on *Chips with
Everything* which were made by leading drama critics in Great
Britain, and I invite the reader to study the back pages of this
volume. However, some of the critics deserve more than the passing reference given them in the bibliography, and it is, I believe,
useful and illuminating to call attention to them.

IV *The Critical Response to Chips*

Just as Wesker attacked the Establishment, so has the Establishment responded and reacted to the play. One could almost
have predicted which critics and which newspapers and magazines in England would praise and which would be critical of
Chips with Everything. Kenneth Tynan, for example, who is himself more or less in the same political camp as Wesker, has had the
highest possible praise for *Chips with Everything*. "A gauntlet of
a play has been flung down on the stage of the Royal Court Theatre," he wrote in his review in *The Observer*. He spells this out:
"Its purpose is not to purge us, but to prove that the body politic

needs purging. We are studying a disease; and what matters is not so much the pain it inflicts as the extent to which it is curable.[6]

Tynan, like other critics, makes special references to the finale, in which (after Pip yields to the pressure of the officers) the entire group of conscripts stands at attention to the national anthem, but the audience remains seated. Ossia Trilling has reported that "it is probably the only play to be performed in Britain in which the National Anthem is played at the climax to an audience so stunned that it does not know whether to take it standing up or sitting down. In fact it remains seated throughout!" [7] Tynan questions this finale, remarking, "I query the resolution." [8] But, by and large, he is highly laudatory and is deeply impressed by the quality of Wesker's language, of which he says that Wesker is no "primitive who has no feeling for words. In fact, he uses them with a secure adroitness that betokens not merely a good ear but a shaping mind and a remarkable flair for character-revealing rhythms." [9]

Kingsley Amis and Bamber Gascoigne, speaking for the Establishment, are strongly critical of *Chips with Everything*. They find little of value in it. Amis is candid enough to confess that he dislikes the entire new English theater: "The whole of the recent renaissance of the English stage is for me a closed book, closed theatre rather. For what it may be worth, though, I will confess further that, from what both friend and foe say of it, the revolution I keep hearing about smells rather like a palace revolution. The many change and pass, the one world of the theatre remains. I am not of it, which makes me impartial." [10] Moreover, Amis admits of Wesker's plays, all of them: "I have never seen any of these works performed," and he says this "even with a touch of legitimate pride"! [11]

Amis does not care for "the curious *patois* spoken by the officers," [12] although he recognizes that it "may serve the purpose of indicating how remote and fantastic, or how nightmarish, these Establishment figures are when properly seen into." [13] He finds Pip lurching "in and out of cumbersome poeticality[14] and refuses to accept the fact that the officers are what he calls "interchangeable phantoms."

Gascoigne, in *The Spectator*,[15] opens his attack by calling *Chips with Everything* "a bad play."[16] He labels Wesker's views as "over-simplified sociology"[17] and "grotesque."[18] He continues his critique:

But this play is not just another version of the Establishment digesting the rebel. Wesker goes much further and questions the nature of all leadership. . . . During his [Thompson's] final speech he changes into officer's uniform, having been, as we now see, a crypto-Gauleiter all along. We are left to assume that no community is tolerable short of the Communist Utopia after the State has finally withered away, but that the vicious cycle of leadership ending always in corruption must make this axiomatically unreachable. The play ends with the ironical blaring of "God Save the Queen" during the triumphal passing-out parade.[19]

Frank McGuinness, in *The London Magazine,* is most caustic. He sneers at Wesker's current high standing as a playwright and tells us that it is quite an experience to see a Wesker play:

The atmosphere of the place is charged with an arch, self-conscious ritualism, a sort of theatre-going manifestation of the political palsy that has in recent years paralysed Left-wing vitality into the posturing attitudes and narcissistic smugness of a fashionable prestige-cult. . . . An air of reverent, collusive expectancy quickly stifles any heretical notion that there is a place here for non-conformist criticism. After all, one doesn't attend High Mass to snipe at the Pope![20]

Speaking for the Establishment, McGuinness denies that Wesker understands his own working class, even though that same class considers Wesker its spokesman. To criticize Wesker, McGuinness claims, "would appear little less than a piece of sacrilegious impertinence, rather as if one were to judge Christ on his merits as a carpenter."[21] Nevertheless, McGuinness isn't frightened by Wesker's high rank among the non-Establishment people. Here is his major attack:

The trouble is that, despite his concern for the working-class and an East End background, Wesker seems to know very little about what makes them tick. Evident enough in his previous plays, it leaps up and screams at us in *Chips with Everything.* Almost totally out touch with the realities of the early sixties, he offers us instead a lesson in sociology which in its over-simplifications, acceptable perhaps thirty years ago, strikes one today as merely ludicrous. A Blimp of the class struggle, he is still flailing away blindly at an enemy who has long since popped underground, changed into mufti and emerged as the smiling unflappable victor of three elections. Indeed, he will, doubtless, put in an appearance at the theatre to applaud the anachronistic antics that assure him that the Socialist imagination is still safely pickled in the twenties. But if the dialectics of the play are irritatingly inept and outdated, the patronizing arrogance of Wesker's I-know-what's-best-for-the-plebs attitude leaves one aching with muscle-taut anger. The idea that one can peddle Culture (by whose definition?) as though it were some health-restoring physic should make the average teacher in the local secondary modern laugh till his next pay rise.[22]

John Russell Taylor, who has written at greater length than any other British critic on Wesker, quotes Wesker's own words in which the playwright states his more recent attitudes on realism. Wesker says:

I have discovered that realistic art is a contradiction in terms. Art is the re-creation of experience, not the copying of it. Some writers use naturalistic means to re-create experience, others non-naturalistic. I happen to use naturalistic means; but all the statements I make are made theatrically. Reality is as misleading as truth; realistic art makes nonsense. If I develop, it might be away from naturalism. I have discovered that this too can be constricting—but I will still be trying to re-create the reality of my experience. I would no more be non-naturalistic for its own sake; I am concerned with both only in order to communicate what experience has meant to me.[23]

Taylor sees in *Chips with Everything* a retreat from naturalism, but he regards the characters in the play as political cartoons. He follows this argument by stating: "Even in a political cartoon a clear grasp of the real facts is required before they can be adapted to the particular requirements in hand. In *Chips with Everything* one is left with the feeling that Wesker has never taken a good, clear look at service life, and so the initial assumption of his allegory based on it is false and all that follows from it is correspondingly suspect. . . ."[24]

Even in a Jewish journal,[25] a Jewish critic,[26] usually friendly towards Wesker's vision, takes issue with the individual tragedy that

Wesker projects: "Pip's submission should be tragic. It fails to be because the author never succeeds in making Pip credible. Thus at the level of social drama, as a study of the R.A.F. machine, this play could hardly be bettered. It hits hard. As the personal tragedy of a rebel swallowed up by the Establishment, however, it fails—because you can't have a personal tragedy unless you have a person." [27]

Clancy Sigal, who has made a reputation in the United States as the author of *Going Away*, has been kinder to Wesker than many of those who have been critical of *Chips with Everything*. He, too, finds elements in it not to his liking, but he recognizes its strengths:

This is Wesker's toughest, most pessimistic play. Its informing idea is simultaneously grand and unthought out, the dialogue some of the best we have had from him, the scenes always taut and absorbing even when inapposite to the central observation. I believe it would have been a more mature and truer play if the main character, Pip, had been a working-class or de-classed rebel and if less of the author's energies had gone into portraying the sheer devilishness (which, of course, is never sheer) of his upper-class targets, the officers. For one thing, Wesker does not really know very much, as indicated in his previous plays, about the upper class as people; he must rely therefore on carica- ture. In a basically non-naturalistic play such as *Chips* this is not a fatal misapprehension. Class domination is a more subtle proposition than Wesker lets on in most of his scenes, although it is obvious, prin- cipally from Pip's lines, that Wesker fully understands this. It is Wes- ker's genius that somehow he manages to discover ways of letting this kind of intellectual over-simplification co-exist with dramatic validity to produce a frequently overwhelming atmosphere of power and ur- gency. I believe this is because his plays are, however they go wrong, psychologically true. And they are true not because he has necessarily discovered a formula—although he is always in some danger of doing this, of borrowing from himself, of vulgarising his fine insights—but be- cause of the majestic moral simplicity with which he unfailingly views social problems and their attachment to the human condition. . . . Wesker is a moral thermometer for the rest of us. Even when he makes us curl up in agonies of embarrassment at his technical gauchness, his over-reliance on sentiment, his youthful evasion or misunderstanding of some nuances while using others to infuse his work, we sense he is almost always saying something terribly important.[28]

With these strictures, the reader may wonder, at times, why Wesker's *Chips with Everything* created such an impact in England and in the United States. If Amis, Gascoigne, and others are correct in their views on Wesker's "false" picture of the Royal Air Force, the upper classes, and even the working class, why has *Chips with Everything* been taken so seriously? True, Sigal calls Wesker "a moral thermometer for the rest of us," [29] but is this enough?

V A Sarcastic Notice

Nigel Dennis, in *Encounter*,[30] a magazine which usually tilts with the Establishment, explains why *Chips with Everything* caught fire. It is, above all, brilliantly staged. It must be remembered that, quite apart from the set speeches and the ideological conflicts, there are scenes in the drama which are sheer action. The drilling; the life in the huts; the bayonet practice; the scene in which the men raid the coke yard—these make for high theatricality. At the same time—no matter what the Establishment critics say about "political cartoons" and "caricatures"—the truth of military pressure to conform comes through strongly.

Dennis' report on *Chips with Everything* is both ironic and sarcastic in the sense that he pretends the play was written by Sergeant-Major Brittain, specialist in the official Manual of Drill, with "additional dialogue" by Arnold Wesker, "the well-known bird watcher." While it is true that Sergeant-Major Brittain had become a legend as a drillmaster, his contribution to *Chips with Everything* was far smaller—to put it clearly—than Dennis seems to believe. In response to my own query on this, Wesker, in a memorandum to me, has stated: "In fact a great deal of the drill was written in by myself and one whole section was discovered by Frank Finlay [one of the stars of the drama] out of the R.A.F. Drill Manual which he learned off by heart and Sergeant-Major Brittain simply took the boys on a number of parades in which he instructed them how to move. He was certainly a great help, but it was John Dexter who gave rhythm to the basic military lessons of Sergeant-Major Brittain."

Yet Dennis writes as though Brittain, not Wesker, were the author of *Chips with Everything*. It is perhaps "clean fun," but it has not amused Wesker. As I quote from Dennis' review, the ironic structure of his essay should be borne in mind; even so, it is obvious that Dennis nevertheless admires much of what is contained in the play. "*Chips with Everything*," Dennis believes, "is a direct reproduction upon a stage of military training as it actually is." [31] Carrying forward his conception, Dennis writes:

In putting it across, Sergeant-Major Brittain laboured under difficulties that would have crushed a playwright. The object of *Chips with Everything* is to show—to *prove*—that the antics of Association Football *are not a necessary consequence of granting privileges to the working class.* Caught young, isolated from their background, and trained properly, youths of *all* classes can be made a credit to their country. But how to prove this? Brittain had behind him many years of experience in dealing with recruits and the Royal Court Theatre allowed him free access to their wardrobe and technical resources. Perhaps he was also helped by the fact that actors nowadays do their utmost to be lifelike and deplore style as a betrayal of honest documentary. But this was all. For the rest, Brittain had nothing to follow but the official Manual of Drill—and this, we suspect, is the only reason why so many people think *Chips with Everything* is a play. For the modern fashion in play-writing is one of direct instruction rather than imaginative appeal, and there could be no better model for this manner than a Forces' handbook. [32]

Yet Dennis does not deny the power of Wesker's idea. While the drilling keeps the audience enthralled and convinces it of the authenticity of the drama, in spite of the "caricatures." Wesker's depiction of the class struggle also remains convincing, and Dennis points to the real reason:

That Pip is marked out for leadership, we never doubt for a moment —and the biggest moment in *Chips with Everything* comes when suddenly we realise *why*. It is because Pip, the gentleman, is the only young man on the stage to whom democracy really means something. Pip, and Pip alone, feels in his heart that the others are his companions —and this regardless of the fact that they are demonstrably *not*. For we are shown very clearly that envy, laziness, obscenity and an immature longing for home are the characteristics of the working class; while in Pip, all such egotism, all conviction that the world was created purely to please Pip, are scorned by him as deleterious, enfeebling and un-Christian. In a very touching passage, Brittain shows this youth wondering whether he should not throw in his lot with the lower classes and, through the doubtful medium of the folk-ballad, lose his identity in theirs. It is his officers who point out to him that such an action would be irresponsible, generous though it might appear. In this neat touch, we see, albeit in miniature, why officers are such a necessary part of an army.

The marvel of *Chips with Everything* . . . is that it succeeds in saying all these important things without ever becoming in the least degree fanciful and intellectual: we can think of no other documentary in which the *simple* truth carries anything like the same burden.[33]

VI *American Praise*

American critics have been far more impressed by *Chips with Everything* than some of the English reviewers, who took as a personal affront Wesker's conception of the Royal Air Force and the British Establishment. The reviewers and critics in the United States were more willing to judge the play as a drama, without bothering too much about the problems that worried Amis, Gascoigne, McGuinness, and the others.

Yet there has been confusion in the United States, too, as to the precise meaning of the play. Walter Kerr has reported: "All the customers I have talked to have liked it, as the reviewers liked it before them. But any one who happened to read all of the notes (only a professional would do such a thing) must have found the confusion fascinating: no two of the reviewers agreed fully on the play's meaning." [34] Quite apart from the various interpretations brought to *Chips with Everything* in the United States, Kerr, for one, enjoyed it:

There is no more exhilarating moment than that in which Pip demonstrates his superior abilities by organizing a happy, even hilarious theft. There is no truer moment than one in which a trainee raises an embarrassing question: what *does* Pip have in mind by deliberately downgrading himself? Author Wesker has never given us a reasonable alternative to this man's advancement; thus, as we watch the final tableau, our eye does not rest on the multiple chins of Old Overflow, it moves across a line of well-drilled (and apparently contented) men to pick out Pip, whose expression betrays nothing but whose whole bearing suggests that he is now precisely where he belongs.[35]

In an earlier review Kerr acknowledges that Americans are bound to view the drama quite differently from the English. "If it is a bit cooler here, emotionally speaking," he remarks, "than it was in Britain, the cause is no doubt to be found in our obvious social differences (I did not say advantages). The reconciliation is undoubtedly moving on home territory; American audiences are less likely to feel themselves immediately involved." [36]

Howard Taubman warns his readers not to consider *Chips with Everything* "crude propaganda." To him, "It has theatrical virtuosity as well as dramatic power and subtlety." [37] To Henry Hewes, the drama is "in some respects a loaded thesis play," [38] but it "is also honest in that the author has set down with accuracy and insight a milieu of which he himself has been a part. And if his officers are a trifle too one-sided, this is balanced by his representation of the enlisted men as somewhat too apathetic and irresolute." [39] To Emory Lewis, *Chips with Everything* is "one of the best plays of the decade," [40] and Wesker "a major twentieth-century dramatist." [41] Harold Clurman,[42] who has some qualifications about the play, nevertheless, considers it more typical of the new English theater than Osborne's *Luther*, and very entertaining. *Newsweek* calls it a play with "stinging immediacy," [43] and *Time* "a scorching fine evening of theatre." [44] Robert Brustein says *Chips with Everything* is "a real development for Wesker who is beginning to grope his way, tentatively and bashfully, towards deeper wells of emotion—if only his awareness were also deeper." [45] Henry Popkin claims that "Wesker too insistently sees himself as a part of the class war, and so he cannot see the rest of it for the purposes of his play." [46]

In the United States, then, *Chips with Everything* was a critical success, and yet it did not run as well in this country as it did in Britain. The class struggle is more relevant to England than it is to Americans. *Chips with Everything* was somewhat alien on these shores, and American audiences—brainwashed to enjoy musicals, or star-studded plays, or plays on sexual conflicts and relationships —did not flock to visit the theater in which *Chips with Everything* was performed. That it ran four months was a triumph of a sort for Wesker's reputation and for the influence of New York reviewers. Social dramas, once common on the American stage, are less so now. Some of the "serious" American playwrights—Williams and Albee, with their sexual torturings—do not deal with political and social issues. Wesker does. Americans seem to want no politics on their stage.[47] It is their loss, for Wesker is dealing with issues that matter—not to Englishmen alone but to all thinking, sophisticated theater-goers. We have them, such theater-goers, but apparently not enough of them today to allow a playwright to become successful when he writes about social issues. *Chips with Everything* has been Wesker's most ambitious produced play, and Clancy Sigal is correct in thinking that Wesker "is on the verge of writing a tremendous play." [48]

CHAPTER 7

Their Very Own and Golden City

ARNOLD WESKER'S most ambitious drama, the one which encompasses almost all of his social ideas, is *Their Very Own and Golden City*,[1] and one cannot resist the temptation of wondering how much of its plotting is dependent upon Wesker's own Centre 42 movement. The reader also cannot help comparing bits and pieces of it to Wesker's earlier plays, in which he invokes William Morris' dreams of a utopian society.[2]

Their Very Own and Golden City is a two-act play. The first act is composed of fourteen scenes. The second act contains six scenes, followed by one continuous scene covering the years from 1948 to about 1990. The play itself begins in 1926. It is full of flashbacks and projections into the future. Some of the scenes are quick, impressionistic, poetic. Others are full of words, words of political passion and violence.

The major protagonist is Andrew Wadham who, as a youngster, dreams of beautiful deeds. He discovers that in order to achieve what he has in mind he must enter the political arena. He becomes a Labour leader, starting with ideals and idealism. Ultimately, he is corrupted by the Establishment and, simultaneously, betrays the working people for whom he ostensibly has always worked. His wife, Jessie, is a simple woman who remains in the background of his life. Kate Ramsey, the daughter of a lord and a lady, is a devil's advocate and serves as his conscience. His three boyhood friends, Paul Dobson,[3] Stoney Jackson, and Jamie Rathbone, grow up into manhood, Dobson as a journalist, Jackson as a minister, and Rathbone as an engineer. They join him in his projects, but cannot truly help him. Jake Latham is a trade union organizer who at first befriends and counsels Andrew, but later is betrayed by him. There are other trade union leaders and industrialists who have their roles to perform, but they seldom come to life. Nevertheless, Wesker's ideas come alive and his passion for social achievements blazes.

In the opening scene, in 1926, Andy, in the company of Jessie, visits Durham Cathedral, and almost his first words in the play are: "Give me love and I'll hate no one. Give me wings and I'll build you a city. Teach me to fly and I'll do beautiful deeds." [4]

Very early in this scene Wesker sets his theme, when he has Andy saying to Jessie:

Supposing you had the chance to build a city, a new one, all the money in the world that you needed, supposing that—this new city—what would you do with it? What would you chuck out, have done with? What new things would you put there? What would you make more important, less important? There it is, all virgin, a new piece of land, lovely, green, rich, what would we do with it? And supposing you had the chance to build six of them, these new cities, and you knew that these cities could set a pattern for all time and, because of that, you realized that there, confronting you, was the opportunity to begin changing the whole way of living for a nation? Supposing that? What would you do?

. . . Supposing you devoted your whole life to it and you began persuading people to collect money, to save it, for their own cities, tens of thousands of people, saving, for their own cities. Supposing that?

I *"Defeat Doesn't Matter"*

Andy has this dream and it remains with him for the rest of his life. What happens to the dream, to Andy, to the people for whom he is striving? That is the story of *Their Very Own and Golden City*. It is, essentially, a tale of failure, but in the words of Jake, the trade union leader, "Defeat doesn't matter. In the long run all defeat is temporary." One believes that Wesker, in creating this plot, in establishing an impossible dream, would rather go down to defeat in his attempt than not dream and try at all.

In the third scene in the first act Andy talks with Jake Latham. Jake, in a long speech, analyzes the failures of Ramsey MacDonald and accuses the Labour leader of having fallen into the Establishment trap. The Bank of England, according to Latham (and, we assume, Wesker) "frightened the pants off" MacDonald. "Would it have been unreasonable to expect a Socialist Government," Latham asks, "to apply Socialist economic principles instead of the usual patchwork?" And Latham offers the "usual" answer, that the Establishment people would say that "the time wasn't ripe."

Then Latham says something that is repeated throughout the drama: "People always need to know that someone was around who acted. Defeat doesn't matter. In the long run all defeat is temporary. It doesn't matter about present generations but future ones always want to look back and know that someone was around acting on principle."

Principles. These are what Andy agonizes over. Kate Ramsey calls herself "a classless woman" and asserts, "I can't bear people who wear their class on their hearts like an emblem." Yet at the end, in the final showdown, Kate is shaken by Andy's compromising and recognizes that "there are casualties on both sides," on the side of the working people and on that of the Establishment, who manipulate the workers. Jake Latham has principles, and he is crushed by Andy in a political fight, based on principles.

Andy wants to build a new Jerusalem and asks, "How, how can we build Jerusalem in England's green and pleasant land?" His friends, Paul Dobson, Stoney Jackson, and Jamie Rathbone, have the proper answers, they think: get rid of rotten housing, and the property owners who built it. The Labour Party is to throw out the property owners—and so it goes, simply, without complications. But life isn't that easy, nor is political maneuvering.

The Labour Party Conference had voted to give strong support to the League of Nations, a move opposed by Latham. This conflict leads to the confrontation between Andy and Latham. It is 1936, with Hitler's power becoming more evident. The debate between the two men permits Wesker to set up the differences between the old, discouraged isolationist, and the young, idealistic internationalist. Latham is unwilling to fight. He is prepared, like the early Christians, to die for his faith, but not to fight.

Latham's argument runs like this:

And now again, in 1936, the same humbugging machinery is in operation, the same appeal to our patriotism is being made. Do we sharpen our knives again? Is that our answer? Everytime, is that going to be our answer? . . . . I am aware that if we do not fight this war then our civilization will enter into terrible times. Terrible times. I know this—I've not loaded the argument on my side; if anything I've done the opposite. But what can an old man do except say the things he passionately believes? Old men have no need to lie, it's all over for them—the days of tactic, of political manoeuvre, of patchwork. . . . I want to say this. Defeat doesn't matter. In the long run all defeat is temporary. . . . I can only tell you that I believe we were intended to live on this earth at peace with one another—if some people do not allow us to do this then I am ready to stand as the early Christians did and say—this is my faith, this is where I stand and, if necessary, this is where I will die.

Andy's attack is easier to comprehend. He points out that the Labour movement has been attacked in every Fascist state and that in most of Europe the unions already have been destroyed. He insists that Latham, by his very call for unity, is cracking the solidarity he wants to maintain.

While these political arguments run throughout the play, Wesker continually emphasizes the dream of the six cities that he desires to build (through Andy), and one cannot stop thinking of Wesker's own plans for Centre 42, with organized cultural festivals throughout Great Britain, under the sponsorship of the trades unions. The concepts are heroic, both the Centre 42 idea and the Golden City concept. Kate, inspired by Andy's ambitions, says, "I'm tired of timid lads who laugh at themselves. I'm tired of little men and vain gestures. I have a need, O God, how I have a need to see someone who's not intimidated. Who'll be heroic again?"

Quite caustically, and honestly, Andy observes, "The hero is a bore." Yet he continues to aim high, in the face of uncertainty. "Yes," he admits, "I'm afraid of failure—petrified. A golden city is a piece of patchwork and patchwork is failure."

II *Complications of a Dream*

As scene 4 in Act II proceeds, the golden cities plan takes on flesh. Andy sees that a single city of one hundred thousand inhabitants would take fifteen years to build and would cost £156,000,-000. Every man would have to find £1,560 for a house for his family and his share of the cost of the communal public building needed for the hundred thousand people living in the city. Andy, as the architect, has his role to play. Jamie will be the civil engineer; Paul, the public relations man; Kate, "the chief bully"; and

Stoney, the representative of God. Kate sneers at the dream. "Look at us," she cries out:

What do you see? A good journalist who might have made a good poet but didn't. Partner number one—frustrated! Terrible credentials. Go home, Paul Dobson. A civil engineer, brilliant innovator but an indifferent idealist! Terrible credentials—go home, Jamie Rathbone. A Dean, a religious administrator, a lover of love who can't bring himself to admit how dulled he is by his experience of it—partner number three. Terrible, terrible credentials—back to your desk, Dean Jackson . . . Me? A daughter of impoverished aristocracy, a woman with a constant sneer in her voice, unloved and with no respect for the will of the people.

Stoney sadly says, "I cannot build your city with the sneers of a dying aristocracy ringing in my ears." Kate replies, "I'm not a dying aristocracy—I'm classless, damn you." Stoney snaps back, "Classless? Classless? The common man would smell you decaying a mile off."
And here Kate speaks in the voice of Wesker:

The common man! The glorious age of the common man! My God, what an age of flabbiness that is. You know, Stoney, it's not really the age of the common man it's the age of the man who is common. . . . Because we need to perpetuate the myth that class differences are past, we pat his head and consult the man who is common in the name of the common man. . . . Architects asking laymen how to build a city. Why shouldn't we turn to you for our homes, to the lawyer for his guidance, to the painter for his art? Would you deny the pastry cook his pleasure to delight you with his craft? Participation? It's a sop, my dear, to ease your conscience.

Andy, listening to the difficulties of building his cities, spells out the work that faces them all. He knows architects and town planners who can establish working committees to find the sites for the cities and draw up the necessary plans for them. He expects to conduct weekly meetings for the first five years to explain the details of the cities and select the right age groups and create the best balance of professions. The applicants would have to begin paying, years in advance, for their homes. It would take eight years before the people would be able to begin to move into their houses. The vision is far-sighted. The plans are tremendous. Men must not be tired. The blood must be young. Andy, as he speaks, grows more and more enthusiastic:

Have we no answer? The most terrible war in history is won—by us—we should be jubilant, we should be singing. We should have answers and not be doubled up by despair. Old men have no answers and when old age is ours then, then we can cry in bewilderment. But now, our blood is young, we should cry—we know! Old age laments, leave lamentations till the grave—*we* know! *We* know what holds men in a movement through all time—it's visions. Visions, visions, visions!

And here he breaks into a form of poetry, into prophecy:

> I tell you,
> this resolution now before you can build a dream. In the
> way you shape a city you shape the habit of a way of life.
>
> I tell you,
> we have a city we can build, we *have* a city.
> We have a city we can build out of whose contours can
> come the breath of such a brave new world.
>
> I tell you,
> The dull and dreary men preach caution, caution is a
> kind of fear, I tell you.
>
> The dull and dreary men breed apathy, apathy is a kind
> of cancer.
> Look, we have a city. But the dull and dreary men—
> beware—
> the dull and dreary men, beware.
> I tell you,
> we have a city, we have a city!

From this point forward, the play becomes a single continuous scene. As Wesker explains it in a "special note": "The long battle to build the city will begin and end in this 'continuous' scene. Towards the end of each situation (set) preparation will be going on for the next situation (set) so that characters will turn immediately from one phase of the development to another. It must appear as one continuous movement, slowly and inexorably unfolding—rather like watching the painting of Dorian Gray slowly change from a young man into an old and evil man—as in the film."

But dreams can fade. What should be the center of the city? What gives it its identity? Wesker asks. What's more important, a concert hall or a tax office? Who is more important, the industrialist or the sculptor? And, of course, the dreamers want everything: gardens, concert halls, dance halls, meeting rooms, libraries, swimming pools, theaters, restaurants, and more, more, always more. Obviously, this has never been done before. But these dreamers believe, at this point, that it can be achieved. Stoney resigns his Deanery. Jamie comes close to divorce. Paul hardly sees his family. Andy himself becomes distant from his wife. And Kate, what has she sacrificed? Her answer is, "Love." So where, then, is the "good life"?

III *Opposition Rises*

The years become harder to live through. Help is not given easily, or gladly or generously. The Government does not give its full support to the scheme. Obstacles continue to rise. It is not an easy job. Money is hard to come by. Industrialists pay lip service to the dream. Trade union leaders question the project each step of the way. One trade unionist observes—as one city begins to take shape—that the trade unions would go bankrupt if they tried to finance six cities. Why not settle for one? he wants to know. The trade union people, it seems, are interested in profits, not dreams. Another trade union leader is cynical and says that Andy really never believed in building six cities. "I mean that's a bit of bargaining power you've set up, isn't it? Give way on the other five and get your own way on one? A bit of market bargaining, eh?"

Andy grows old and tired as he fights everyone. He is told he is not practical. He is asked to compromise. At first he is adamant; then he is maudlin; finally he compromises. He settles for one city, not as he dreamed it would be, but—he tries to convince himself —a start.

Defeated, Andy is now made Sir Andrew Wadham. The Establishment has won out and, in winning, offers Andy a title, fine and high-flown words, praise glibly spoken. The years have passed, for it has taken fifteen years to build the one Golden City. In responding to those who attempt to honor him, Andy replies: "I'm honoured and I'd be churlish and ungracious not to be—yes, churlish and ungracious not to be. After all—the Golden City is built, there were compromises, but it's built, a hint, if nothing else, of what might be."

Yet he realizes he has been beaten:

> Where are the flowers? I don't smell flowers.
> They'll wait another twenty years and then another leader will
> come along and they'll build another city. That's all.
> Patchwork! Bits and pieces of patchwork.
>
> It was all patchwork. Six cities, twelve cities—what
> difference. Oases in the desert, and soon the sun would
> dry them up and the sands would cover them.
>
> But who can tell them that? I can't tell them that, I don't want
> to talk, me.
>
> Nor listen. I don't want to listen either. I never did.
> Not even to myself. Patchwork—one city, six, twelve,
> what difference? And I didn't listen—silly old fool.

Wesker makes the point even clearer, when he has Harrington, the industrialist, inform Andy: "Your boys want a better standard of living? Good, they can have it. First-aid kits in their factories, flush lavatories, sanitary conditions? Good, they can have them." Maitland, the Minister of Town and Country Planning, digs deeper: "The odd Golden City or two? We'll build them, we'll help you even. But we rule and we need prefects, your life-long boys supply them." Harrington adds: "We employ and we need employees, your life-long boys provide them." Maitland chimes in: "And when it's necessary—we knight you. . . . Are you still in the age of the common man, Andy? Still on about democracy? There's no such thing as democracy, dear boy, simply a democratic way of manipulating power, you should know that."

Finally, even with one Golden City established, Andy knows that he has been had, that he could not win, that he has fought against the "interests," not only the bankers and the industrialists and the politicians, but his own trade union people—and all unified against him. They threw him a handful of bones and knighted him and permitted him his symbol of a single city. But only because it helped *them*, the members of the Establishment. There is the freedom to have visions, but not to carry them out.

"Defeat doesn't matter": we hear this refrain throughout the play. But doesn't it? "All defeat is temporary in the long run." But is it? We are left with the question and we have the freedom to find our own answers.

Their Very Own and Golden City is a lengthy, complex drama with many powerful sequences, biting speeches, bewildered complaints and wailings. It is panoramic, deep in its implications, and apparently difficult and complicated to stage. But it is typical of Wesker's work and attitude toward society. At a time when most of his contemporaries shy away from political and social plays, he adamantly continues to probe the ills of his society and is unafraid of the challenges both of presenting his political views and of making a theatrical work from them. He remains undefeated.

CHAPTER 8

The Four Seasons

AFTER having written *Their Very Own and Golden City*, Wesker undertook a totally different kind of drama, one radically different from anything else he has done. It has practically no "social significance"; it is not elaborately staged; it is almost entirely nonpolitical.[1] To the extent that it is, at heart, the story of a romance that fails, it is reminiscent of *Roots*. But while Beatie Bryant and Ronnie Kahn of *Roots* had mixed politics with passion, social awareness with flesh, this new play, *The Four Seasons*, is suggestive of an Existentialist play. Hopelessness, pessimism, the lack of communication between lovers—these are its major elements. And, like so many recent dramas, it attempts to probe deeply—on a stage that is practically bare, and with only two characters, a man and a woman. There is, as Wesker phrases it, "only one, long continuous act." And he offers his actors this bit of advice, "Would actors kindly not take a curtain call on this occasion."

The play begins during the winter, and the scenes then blend into the seasons that naturally follow. Adam and Beatrice are "between thirty and thirty-five years old." They have entered a deserted house and, it slowly develops, they have come here for a year, to prove their love for one another. Beatrice has been married and divorced, and she has taken a lover. Adam has left his wife and children.

There is little action throughout the play. The man and woman attempt to decorate the house. They paint it. Some cooking and baking are done. They talk; they argue; they torture one another; and at the end of the year, with the passage of the four seasons, they have found no solace in one another. Their problems have not been solved. It is a play with little stage business, with some long speeches and with unutterable sadness. Wesker is obviously trying to probe the psyches of contemporary man and woman in the civilized world. He is wondering why an adult, human relationship is so hard to achieve. From time to time the speeches read like formal essays, and yet eloquence breaks through. The drama is not very dramatic; the characters are not sharply drawn. Yet the play nags at the mind and the heart.

In the beginning of the year's experiment Adam is eager to do all he can for Beatrice. "For the first weeks," he tells her, "I'll prepare everything for you. Make your food, your bed, warm you. Just for the first weeks." Nevertheless, he shies away from the concept of love. He has found love painful. During the entire first scene Adam does all the talking. His is the only voice heard in the second scene. Beatrice is silent until the third scene. But much has been established through Adam's words.

He tells the quiet Beatrice that he will do things for her, but he won't love her. "Not love again. Not all that again. I'll give you human warmth but not human love. Not that again. Not all those old, familiar patterns of betrayal again, those approaches." He is afraid of love, and he predicts that, when the year is over, she might say that nothing has truly happened. They would give their hearts to one another—and only emptiness would result.

It is clear that, in her silence, Beatrice is suffering, and enjoying the act of suffering. She is not only silent, but morbid, self-pitying, lifeless.

This does not seem like a promising start for an exciting play. The drama begins to move, however, as the lovers talk, as their problems take shape before the eyes. As spring commences, Beatrice comes to life. She garlands her lover with bluebells. Her skin is now soft and her eyes are confident. Adam wants her to remain alert and loving. Perhaps, he thinks, something will come of their attachment. He is willing to offer her the world. "Just ask," he pleads with her. But, as they talk, her voice turns sharp. She has been hurt in the past and is unsure of Adam. "Doesn't pessimism ever lose its attraction for you?" he wonders. "Do you prefer morbidity?"

I *Failures and Defeats*

The defeats suffered by Beatrice have colored her attitudes. Gradually some of the experiences of her past life are revealed. She has had a bad marriage: "Do you know what my husband once said to me? 'You're like a queen,' he said, 'without a country. I hate queens without their country.'" This theme is repeated throughout the play. Her husband had made her feel indifference, and she despised him for it. And her lover, who had been "a leader of men," had not been indifferent, but she had failed him.

Adam's failures had been less obvious, but he says, "I have a desperate need to give joy, to create laughter again, to heal someone." The sadness is that, in the end, he does not give joy or create laughter. Beatrice had said to him, "I need to be healed . . . I'm tired of the sound of my own voice. I need to be healed, I've destroyed a marriage and failed a lover—I need to be healed." But Adam cannot heal her.

They labor at creating a life, a world, of their own. They whitewash the walls of the deserted house. They shop for "things." They discuss their talents. Adam has danced, and plays instruments, and weaves tapestries full of fantasies. Beatrice has a half-finished novel. She does not paint, but she has known painters. She does not write poetry, but she has known people who have read her their poems. She has been barren, and she cannot sing. Adam tries to teach her to sing, to voice a melody. He cannot believe that she is unable to do so. "Everybody can sing," he insists. But Beatrice is incapable of song. She cannot produce sweet notes.

The symbolism here is clear, hammered home by Wesker. "Everybody sings," Adam repeats. "It's not like having eyes, or being lame. What do you do with babies if you can't lullaby them? What sound do you make when you smell the first flowers?" In agony, Beatrice replies, "I can't, I can't, that's it, I can't. No sound, I make no sounds, just a long moan, or a silence." And then the refrain, "I destroyed a marriage and failed a lover . . ."

She tells Adam of her lover, the "leader of men." She failed him because of her intense jealousy. When he sat quietly and she wanted to know what he was thinking about, he would say, "My mind's a blank," and she would not believe him. She could not bear his children. Her love for him—and his for her—was deep, too deep. They communicated well. But too great a love was too much for them, and she cannot forgive herself. As she explains the violent love of her past, she bares her body to Adam, and as the spring passes, they make love to one another.

For the moment their love glows. Beatrice becomes poetic, lyrical in her passion. "When you need me to be your sun," she promises him, "I'm your sun. When you need soft winds I shall cover the land with my breath. When you need comfort then I shall offer my breasts and my limbs and my lips. Whatever you call for you shall have." She calls Adam her "golden eagle." And, suddenly, love has made her whole, and young, and she believes in everything. "I would like to be young again for you; I would like to be shy and pure and untouched for you. I blush for the creases in my skin, I'm ashamed of my worn limbs and crippled senses. I feel fresh while the air is fresh but once the winter comes I'll remember the staleness of my body."

The dialogue here becomes almost embarrassingly naive as Beatrice articulates her feelings. It reads a bit like second-rate D. H. Lawrence, and one begins to wonder whether the entire play will stumble along in this fashion. But it changes. Wesker turns away from the bald poetry and makes the long set remarks by Adam—when he then tells Beatrice of his relationship with his wife—credible. Her love was oppressive. She was possessive and could not forgive Adam for his gift of laughter. As a result, she became a lonely woman, and yet he missed her. "With her the laughter turned into cries of pain; without her the laughter is gone. We never really recover."

As she listens to Adam, Beatrice herself turns cold and venomous, possessive and cruel. She is unwilling to hear the truth of the past. She rejects candor, for she wants to enclose herself with him, away from the rest of the world. Adam recognizes that "there's a war on between us. . . . All the time, a war, and it goes on and on and I try to believe it can't be true, not all the time, but it is."

II Conflict in the Open

The conflict is out in the open. They are both flawed, blemished. They have gone away together; they have shared their bodies; but they are damaged souls. In the midst of their snarling, Adam collapses, and Beatrice cares for him over a period of weeks. Meanwhile, she talks to and at him (as he did to her in the opening scene), and she regrets her life, her attitudes, her failures. She reflects, as Adam lies motionless, "I'm damaged, second hand.

Third hand to be precise; third hand, bruised and damaged—like a clock striking midnight when the hour is only six, and it wheezes and whirs. But the hands always point to the right time. And if we had met each other before we had met anyone else, then the hands would have pointed to the right time and the right hour would have sung clear and ringing."

The conflicts continue when Adam recovers. For a time, they are content. There is a scene during which they prepare to make apple strudel.[2] Yet, even in this moment of accomplishment, they cannot get along. Adam laughs with pleasure and Beatrice admits, "I can't bear your laughter, it's unnatural. It casts everybody out." She resents his laughter; she seeks to possess him, as his wife before her had done. And Adam responds by saying that Beatrice, like all women, is capable of abuse. Again they flay one another as they talk about their past relationships. She had merely stopped loving her husband and Adam had felt guilty over his treatment of his wife, who left him for another man. As they confide in one another, they discover they no longer need one another. They cannot recover from their pasts. Beatrice continues to display her jealousy; Adam, his guilt. They accuse each other of being incapable of love. They are exposed. "We weren't even really friends, were we?" Beatrice asks. And Adam admits, "No."

"It's always foolish," Adam declares toward the end of the play, "to try and know more than one person. To know more than one person is to betray them." Beatrice answers. "On the contrary, to know only one person is to betray the world." And Adam, continuing the dialogue, observes:

Do you think that when the millenium comes there will not be lovers who grow weary of their sad girls, or that wives will not weep over empty beds? Even when Jerusalem is built, friends will grow apart and mothers will mourn their sons growing old. Do you want me to feel for starving children? I feel for them. Do you want me to protest at wars that go on in the mountains? I protest. But the heart has its private aches. You must allow the heart its private aches.

Thus the two lovers, who could not find comfort in one another, tear at one another and lose confidence in themselves. Sometimes *The Four Seasons* reads like a debate between a man and a woman; at other moments it illuminates truths and comes to life.

[89]

It does not have the bitterness of Edward Albee's *Who's Afraid of Virginia Woolf?* Nor does it possess the sickness of the confrontations in some of the plays of Tennessee Williams. In its tearing, probing, pain-inflicting scenes, it is not unlike Murray Schisgal's *Luv.*

Nonetheless, although it lacks both humor and clear character portrayal, and is talkative, as any two-person drama must be, it is an interesting experiment and has passages of insight that are poetic and bitter-sweet. Wesker, in much of his work, is an optimist, although in both *The Four Seasons* and *Their Very Own and Golden City* that optimism is submerged and even repressed. *Chips with Everything* was basically a play which recognized the hopelessness of a given situation (fighting the Establishment), but realized the fight was worth making. In *The Four Seasons* Wesker has restricted himself to a narrow, but meaningful, conflict: the war between the sexes. It is not "clever" or amusing. It is thoughtful and it reverberates in the mind. It remains with the reader. At this writing, it has not been staged, but one can predict that, if well done (and it would have to be a *tour de force*), it could be memorable theater. It is a departure for a social playwright, and it is not entirely in the style of the earlier Wesker. Yet it reaches for meanings, it tries to say something important, and it is serious, as is characteristic of the work of Arnold Wesker.

CHAPTER 9

Pools *and* Menace

WESKER writes primarily for the stage; he thinks in terms of the living theater. But, like many creative and literary men, he tries his skill in other mediums as well. He has produced some poetry, a few impressionistic sketches of life in London, and a sheaf of book reviews, none of which warrants extended analysis. There are, however, two longer works by Wesker which help to illuminate his view of individuals and society. They are skillful and thoughtful, and, although they are not major works by any means, they deserve more than passing reference. Early in his career, Wesker wrote a long short story entitled *Pools*,[1] which attracted the attention of Lindsay Anderson, and, after *Chips with Everything*, Wesker accepted the challenge of a new form, the television drama. In *Menace* he has not succeeded in producing a memorable play, yet it has its special interest. "The medium of television," he writes, "is quite different from that of the theatre and when asked to write a play especially for television I was anxious to approach it in a completely different way. *Menace* is an exercise as much as anything else . . ."[2]

I A Story of Illusions

Pools is the story of a fifty-five-year-old Jewish widow named Mrs. Hyams. She is one of the nameless "little people" of London's East End. She lives alone. Her married daughter lives in Bermuda, and her son visits her only once a week. Isolated as she is, Mrs. Hyams retains relationships with some of her elderly neighbors. She visits Mrs. Levy, who is sixty years old and a former beauty. The two old ladies discuss their families and talk of Passover and of Jewish foods like chopped liver and borsht. Mrs. Hyams pities Mrs. Levy, for she recalls when her friend had been the reigning belle of the neighborhood. Mrs. Levy's husband "had treated her as a princess; he did the shopping, the cooking, the housework." He died when she was thirty, and Mrs. Hyams, remembering the earlier, happier days, has vast sympathy for her friend.

The story begins as though it were going to be merely another tale of Jewish nostalgia, family relationships, and old age, but it is not. It is, instead, a study of insecurity and obsession, of shattered dreams and illusions.

Mrs. Hyams is obsessed with football pools. Each week she fills out her football coupon from the newspaper, hoping to win £75,-000. What would she do with the money? She compiles a list and mulls over it, taking pleasure in her chore. She would buy a house for her children and their families so that she and they could live under one roof. She would, if necessary, support them. She would give money to her three brothers and to her friends. She would buy "a pair of fur-lined boots for winter" and would spend £20 "on a holiday in a little seaside village." And, after she has felt sorry for Mrs. Levy, she thinks of giving the lonesome old lady £25,000.

Wesker describes how the pools give meaning and substance and security to her life:

When her husband was alive nothing used to irritate Mrs. Hyams more than Wednesday night, pools' night. Every week he would ask her to write it out for him because he was afraid of making a mistake; every week he asked her whether or not he should change the numbers he used. "Will Stockport and Wolves draw, do you know?" he would ask. "If I knew," she replied, "I'd tell you, fool!" When her husband died her boy took to doing the pools, but he married at nineteen and spent his first five married years abroad in the army. Soon afterwards her daughter married. In a short, perplexing period of time her whole family, the point of her existence, had broken up. It was some years before she regained her self-possession. Time and routine hardened her; Life moved in her despite herself. She forced pleasures in trivialities, making do with the remains. Soon the sense of loyalty with which she took up the pools gave way to a sense of imperativeness. She must win the pools because with this money she would piece together the ruins of her family. This gave to her a calm such as a wonderful secret can give; a calm disturbed only by loneliness, when she would hurry to her brothers or a friend.

Mrs. Hyams, enraptured by the pools, continues to fill out the coupons without ever winning. Finally, her neighbors, in appreciation for her help during many winters, collect £20 for her so that she can take a holiday. Thus one of her dreams comes to fruition. She goes to a seaside village on the north coast of East Anglia. She loves the salt air, the peacefulness, the narrow, cobbled streets. Her hosts are pleased that the elderly lady is enjoying herself.

On a Sunday morning, Mrs. Hyams wakes up and, after being served breakfast, notices that the Sunday newspaper she had ordered is not available. It seems that there is no newspaper. How can she check her pools, to discover if she has won? She rushes to the village for a newspaper but cannot find one. "In the indolence of the country she had been too free, intoxicated with the freshness of her change. At home she could rely on life, here nothing mattered." She keeps searching, searching until she finds a newspaper—which she proceeds to lose in the bus while she is returning to her room. She panics and decides to go back to London. The trip is long. But even in London there is no newspaper—it is late in the evening. "Had London gone mad not to have news?"

Mrs. Hyams decides to send a telegram to the pools, claiming she has won, but the process of contacting the proper office bewilders her and she almost gives up—until she notices a front and back page of a newspaper on the ground. She stoops to pick it up and rushes to the women's toilet to check her pools. "Carefully she folded the newspaper leaving in sight in the smallest space possible all the results she wanted. Then, withdrawing a yellow pencil from her handbag, she checked, one by one, the entries of her coupon." She has not won anything. "Why," she asks herself, "should Mrs. Hyams win £75,000 anyway?" She concludes, "She's no one. So? Nu?"

Seemingly, Mrs. Hyams is an eccentric, a lone woman with her private dreams. But Wesker claims: "This woman represents millions in England." [3] And once again the author captures on paper the lonely, alien members of society, who dream wildly, meaninglessly.

Mrs. Hyams is a dreamer, as are so many of Wesker's characters. Pip in *Chips with Everything*, while an idealist, is also a dreamer. So is Beatie Bryant in *Roots*, and so, too, are Dave and

Ada, the young couple in *I'm Talking About Jerusalem,* who seek a life of idealism in the country, away from the grinding harshness of metropolitan life. *Pools* contains some of the themes and attitudes which we later find more clearly and powerfully expressed in Wesker's more ambitious dramas.

II *The Dispossessed of the World*

Menace, which is loaded with trivialities, nevertheless contains a few powerful scenes and passages and is recognizably Wesker in its more eloquent passages. The entire television play deals with a group of people who live in a shabby apartment house. Again, Wesker depicts the dispossessed of the world. Sophie, an old woman who inhabits a basement room, is slowly going blind, and has a cat for a companion. Maxie is a thirty-five-year-old neurotic who, like Mrs. Hyams, fills out the football pool coupons. Daphne, a middle-aged woman, is continually writing letters to influential Englishmen in the hope that they will help to commute her brother Sammy's prison sentence. Garry is a twenty-two-year-old artist who, as the play opens, is entertaining his mistress, Harriet.

All the tenants are friendly with one another; Harriet is the outsider. Sophie, Maxie, and Daphne intrude on the young couple, who have recently made love. They all talk about minor matters. They are poor; they are unwilling to face life. And when Harriet, who has money, invites them all out to dinner, they accept the invitation as a great adventure. In the restaurant Garry and Harriet bicker over what to order. It becomes a grim game, and the observer realizes that the young couple are tense, unsure with each other, seeking no one knows what. The restaurant scene, which does not appear in the first version, has been written into the television script. It adds little, but it reminds one that Wesker, who had worked in a restaurant kitchen, knows something about ordering food.

Wesker himself sees symbolic meaning in the stage business— the ordering of and concentrating on food. "This indicates," he insists, "as most of the other scenes attempt to indicate, the way in which people begin things they never finish. It is a play about insecurity, about a threatened world that menaces our security so that we never have a chance to develop fully, to finish things!" [4]

As the five people leave the restaurant, they pick up three

young boys and bring them to their apartment house. There seems to be no reason for the introduction of the youngsters, except to indicate that the five major characters cannot communicate with them. Eventually, the boys leave; from time to time the others talk about life, politics, love, and health. Garry is sarcastic when he hears a radio announcer report that the premier of the country insists that the nation has "a duty to the two million people in West Berlin." Maxie snarls that he is a victim of the system, that, if he borrows money, he will always remain in debt. Daphne is, as she herself acknowledges, a "nasty old woman" who wishes her old age on the young lovers. Sophie stumbles her way through life, hardly able to see, the world a blur.

Garry and Harriet torture each other; they are unhappy together and unhappy apart. "We pretend to be sophisticated," Garry says, but it is clear that they are not. They threaten to leave each other, but this, too, they are unable to do. Toward the end of the play Garry complains:

The way we talk off the top of our heads. Why can't you leave? What is there that stops you leaving? You know how it'll end, and you know that we'll row and cut each other to pieces so what holds you? Not the room, there's nothing beautiful about the room, there's no rest here. Not me, there's nothing beautiful about me. Does it ever occur to you how unbeautiful you are? Have you ever known a generation to be as unbeautiful and mediocre as we are? Self conscious, timid, faceless— content with little, little, little bits of experience.

In this passage there are echoes of Beatie Bryant and Pip and other Wesker rebels. Garry challenges Harriet and asks her, "What is the grandest most glorious thing you've ever done?" and Harriet replies weakly, "One day—I left home." Garry sneers "Huh! Left home! She left home, he told his teacher where to get off, she told her boss to stick his job up his jumper, he told the policeman to mind his own business, she joined a march to protest against tests, he joined a demonstration against unemployment. Little, little, little bits of experience."

In this fashion the young lovers tear at each other and question the value of their society and their lives. They nevertheless continue to dream, and Garry recalls how he once was one of a group that showed paintings and read poems before workers in a factory. At first the workers refused to listen to the poetry readings. "A thousand men and women, freed from the noise of their machines, clattering their cutlery, busily shouting the day's gossip at each other" ignored Garry. He remembers that the indifference almost destroyed him. But then he tried a second factory. "This time we made our arrangements through the shop stewards who presented us before an audience of four hundred after they'd eaten, and we were listened to and applauded. . . ."

These are the final words of the play. As Garry and Harriet walk toward a basement where they hear the music of a Rumanian folk dance and see young people enjoying themselves, the viewer sees Garry and Harriet enter and the play ends on a note of some hope. The people can be made to listen. Again there are echoes of *Chips with Everything* and of *Roots.* Wesker, even in a television play, a new medium for him, is unwilling to forget that he is a man with a cause.

Menace was not particularly well received by the critics, although, curiously, John Russell Taylor, who frequently has been critical of Wesker, gave it high marks. He liked *Menace* "better than anything else he has written." [5] His reasons are lucid enough, even if not persuasive. "For once," Taylor writes of Wesker, "it seemed to me, this was properly speaking and all the way through a play: never did one get the uncomfortable feeling that the words we were hearing were not those of the character, but those of Mr. Wesker speaking through a mouthpiece, directing what we should think. For the first time he has sought simply to present us with a group of unpredictable, contradictory characters thrown together in certain circumstances and reacting as they would react to those circumstances and to each other. He has not dotted i's and crossed t's, he has not made anyone represent anything except himself or herself, he has given us no causes. . . . Mr. Wesker now appreciates that if people *want* chips (or baked beans) with everything this is a reaction just as genuine, and just as much respected, if not agreed with, as any other." [6]

In spite of Taylor's pleasure over Wesker's abandonment of his recurrent themes, those themes remain in *Menace,* just as they recur in all of Wesker's plays, stories, and interviews. He is clearly trying to do more than entertain. He is trying to make one think, to wake one up.

CHAPTER 10

Centre 42

IN all of Wesker's work there is reflected an anguished spirit. Wesker has never been satisfied merely with writing dramas for the sake of success and affluence. He is part of a movement in Great Britain which is idealistic, which seeks to "improve" the cultural patterns of the people of the nation.

Bernard Kops, himself a dramatist of importance and influence, and the author of *The Hamlet of Stepney Green* and *The Dream of Peter Mann*, has declared that "the working classes have become articulate and young writers have sprung up all over the country, products of this special time, symptomatic of the great social changes that have taken place, perhaps the first bubbles of a mighty volcano." [1] He explains the situation, in England and in drama, in these more specific terms:

Theatre in England is no longer the precious inner sanctum for the precious few. Writers such as Shelagh Delaney, John Arden, Arnold Wesker, Alun Owen, Robert Bolt, Willis Hall and myself have changed the face of things and we hope for all time. We write about the problems of the world today because we live in the world of today. We write about the young, because we are young. We write about Council flats and the H-bomb and racial discrimination because these things concern us and concern the young people of our country, so that if and when they come to the theatre, they will see that it is not divorced from reality, that it is for them, and they will feel at home. [2]

Wesker himself has expressed his theories about mass culture and the "improvement" of it in his celebrated final scene in *Roots*. Beatie Bryant, in her explosive statement of self-discovery, cries out: "Education is not only books and music—it's asking questions, all the time. There are millions of us, all over the country and no one, not one of us is asking questions, we're all taking the easiest way out. We don't fight for anything, we're so mentally lazy we might as well be dead." Then follows the biting and eloquent conclusion of Beatie's speech:

Do you think we really count? You don' wanna take any notice of what them ole papers say about the workers bein' all important these days—that's all squit! 'Cos we aren't. Do you think when the really talented people in the country get to work they get to work for us? Hell if they do! Do you think they don't know we 'ont make the effort? The writers don't write thinkin' we understand, nor the painters don't paint expecting us to be interested—that they don't, nor don't the composers give out music thinking we can appreciate it. "Blust," they say, "the masses is too stupid for us to come down to them. Blust," they say, "If they don't make no effort why should we bother?" So you know who come along? The slop singers and the pop writers and the film makers and women's magazines and the Sunday papers and the picture strip love stories—that's who come along, and you don't have to make no effort for them, it come easy. "We know where the money lie," they say, "Hell we do! The workers've got it so let's give them what they want. If they want slop songs and film idols we'll give 'em that then. If they want words of one syllable, we'll give 'em that then. If they want the third rate, BLUST! We'll give 'em THAT then. Anything's good enough for them. 'Cos they don't ask for no more!" The whole stinkin' commercial world insults us and we don't care a damn. Well, Ronnie's right—it's our own bloody fault. We want the third-rate —we got it!

Although this passage is the highlight of *Roots*, its words go beyond both the printed page and the stage. In an essay in *Encounter*,[3] on Centre 42, Wesker observes that "these words are given to the characters in my plays. They are not simply bits of dialogue designed to give body to the work, not simply ideas I hand on indifferently to those characters. They are thoughts that have seared across my mind. What must I do now? Is it enough to write them and help them on to a stage? How must I conduct the rest of my life? Have holidays in the South of France, amuse my friends at parties, rear children, vote, give talks on theatrical history? What can those words have meant to me if that is all I do once they are written?" Wesker has gone far beyond the words. After *Chips with Everything* was produced, he abandoned play-

writing to devote himself full-time to the management of Centre
42.

I *What Is Centre 42?*

What is Centre 42, how did it begin, what is Wesker's involve-
ment in it, and what does it portend for the future? In 1960 Wesker, already famous at twenty-eight as the author of *Chicken
Soup with Barley* and *Roots*, gave a talk, before a group of stu-
dents at Oxford University, in which he complained about contemporary British culture. Obviously, this lecture hit a nerve and,
as Charles Marowitz reported, "Before long, a group of interested
British artists met in conclave to fashion a weapon with which to
combat the forces that were merchandizing and vulgarizing art in
Britain." [4] This group of writers, designers, television producers,
actors, publishers, journalists, and directors met, talked, and argued. At a Trades Union Congress on the Isle of Man in September, 1960, The Association of Cine and Television Technicians put
forward a resolution which was passed at the Congress as Resolution 42. It read as follows:

Congress recognises the importance of the arts in the life of the community especially now when many unions are securing a shorter working week and greater leisure for their members. It notes that the trade
union movement has participated only to a small extent in the direct
promotion of plays, films, music, literature and other forms of expression including those of value to its beliefs and principles.
Congress considers that much more could be done and accordingly
requests the General Council to conduct a special examination and to
make proposals to a future Congress to ensure a greater participation
by the trade union movement in all cultural activities. [5]

Centre 42 was conceived to implement and realize the aims of
this resolution. A brochure issued by the Centre 42 movement
states, in idealistic terms, and with passion:

Centre 42 will be a cultural hub which, by its approach and work,
will destroy the mystique and snobbery associated with the arts. A
place where artists are in control of their own means of expression and
their own channels of distribution; where the highest standards of pro-

fessional work will be maintained in an atmosphere of informality; where the artist is brought into closer contact with his audience enabling the public to see that artistic activity is a natural part of their daily lives.

The confusion of our cultural and social scene is partly the result of an inability to distinguish between standards and prejudices; it is a scene where the young people in new communities can find no roots; where artists feel it neither necessary nor possible to make contact with their public. Sociological and economic factors are the causes of this confusion: age-old prejudices and a crippling commercial system based on appeal to the lowest standards for the quickest and safest financial returns.

The FORTYTWO movement is a bid by a new generation of writers, actors, musicians, painters, sculptors, architects to relieve commercial managements of the burdens and responsibilities in shaping our culture; to assume this responsibility themselves and place art back into the lap of the community where, through familiarity and participation, they can revitalise their work by confronting a new audience and turn their art from a purposeless mess into a creative force.[6]

Charles Marowitz spells it out in even more forceful terms, although throughout the phraseology the words of Beatie Bryant come through:

It was to decentralize the theatre; to nourish the provinces and backwaters of England which had for so long been cut off from first-class art; to renounce the creed by which art had become synonymous with commodity and formularized for mass consumption. It refused to accept that most invidious and ironclad of all principles: that the commercial powers which bought, sold and packaged the work of artists had an inalienable right to it. It declared instead that art belonged to the artist; that the profiteer, the ten-percenter, and the backroom boys simply did not figure in the process; that art was the joint property of the creator and his public and that when this partnership was observed, the quality of art would improve—as would the size of the public and, in time, its taste.[7]

Before Centre 42 could carry forward its plans (to obtain a multipurpose building; to set up "working parties to find and work out new ideas"),[8] a small city in Northern England, Wellingborough, asked Centre 42 to help it mount its annual arts festival.

[100]

Wesker reported that "without money and organization we accepted the challenge and the result proved a landmark." [9] Five people went to Wellingborough and worked there for eight days. Apparently it was more successful than the dreamers dreamed. Trades councils in Bristol, Hayes, Leicester, Birmingham, and Nottingham extended similar invitations to Centre 42. Clearly, Centre 42 was in business. The union with the trade union movement was quite natural. Wesker makes it clear:

In order to explain Centre 42 we must look at the problems confronting another movement—the trade union movement. They have a problem similar to that of the artist: the problem of an indifferent public. The members they have are losing interest in "the literature of the rule book and the arts of negotiation" and the cry is going up from old members that "there are no young people to take our place." The way in which they are beginning to answer this problem is to hold "Trade Union Weeks"—a mixed bag of events from lectures on the industrial health service to mannequin parades and folk-singing evenings.[10]

II *Some Achievements*

As an example of what Centre 42 has done, it is instructive to study the brochures of the festivals at Bristol and at Leicester. The festival at Leicester was particularly exciting. It was held in that city from October 7 through October 13, 1962. There was presented *Enter Solly Gold,* a new drama by Bernard Kops; a jazz concert; Theatre Folk Ballad, featuring "The Lonesome Train," by Millard Lampell and Earl Robinson, and "The Maker and the Tool," specially written for the festival by Charles Parker and utilizing documentary tape recordings of working people in the cities where the festivals were being held. In addition, there were local art exhibitions by both adults and children; folk music concerts with Peggy Seeger, Ewan MacColl, A. L. Lloyd, and a score of other artists and groups; poetry readings; a musical theater featuring work by Igor Stravinsky. The program in Bristol and in the other cities was much the same.

The Centre 42 program is ambitious and far-reaching. It has had its critics as well as its warm friends. Charles Marowitz has said that "what worries me about the Centre and its ideas is the assumption that working-class art is going to be superior to the best commercial art," [11] and he reports that "many of the architects of Centre 42 feel the whole project is too massive and that if its sights were lowered more could be achieved." [12] Nevertheless, mixed with his own criticism is a pat on the back:

In its most disturbing aspects, Centre 42 smacks of the old nineteenth-century idea of "elevating the working classes." Instead of blue-blooded altruists, one finds militant socialist-intellectuals . . . to justify itself, the Centre must provide art which is as good as or better than that being offered by the Establishment outlets. This they have not yet done and will find difficulty in doing. (It may be significant that when the Centre approached leading British playwrights for new festival plays, they received a wave of negative replies—even from such sympathizers as Osborne, Harold Pinter, John Whiting, Arden and Robert Bolt.) So far the Centre's social intentions tend to overwhelm pure artistic considerations, and one worries about the sold neo-realistic bias in the group's organizers. If the new audience is to be flooded with the old chestnuts of problem-plays, the British theatre may well be coaxed out of a *cul-de-sac* and into a back alley.

But these are niggling reservations. If Centre 42 expands and prospers, it can do nothing but good.[13]

Jennie Lee, a member of Parliament, a member of the Centre 42 Committee,[14] and the widow of Aneurin Bevan, in a letter published in *Encounter,*[15] offers her tribute to Wesker, his aggressiveness, and his idealism. It is worth reprinting, for it expresses the view not only of a woman powerful within the Labour Party but of one who, at the outset, saw the entire scheme as somewhat outlandish:

Arnold Wesker has got hold of a brave idea. When I first heard him talk about it I felt guilty and embarrassed. Ought I to share all this burning faith? Did he really think the trade union movement was capable of accepting his challenge? It seemed to me that he knew very little about it. I could see headaches and heartaches ahead for him.

But I suppressed my cynical unbelief. Or at least, I suppressed a good deal of it, throwing out just one or two warning hints, no more.

After all, let him find out for himself. No, that was not really my attitude. Rather it was a sad hope that his faith might make us whole. He did not know our shortcomings. He did not have a clinical close-up. His was the poet's vision, a kind of inspired lunacy.

So why not tag along for a bit, if not able to do very much to help, at least not hindering.

[102]

It was pretty much in that mood that I accepted an invitation to become a member of the "Centre 42" Committee.

Shortly afterwards I met Joan Littlewood and as on all things, she had a positive, vehement point of view. She said, "It takes ten or eleven years to make a good playwright. That is Arnold's job, and he should stick to it." Clearly it was protective goodwill towards an able young artist that prompted her to say so. We all know there is a job for the carthorse and a job for the racehorse. Why should not someone less gifted do the footwork, the slogging, all the tedious and exhausting organisation chores?

I took the point and did not press my own, which is, simply, that when a hazardous new venture is being launched it needs speed, it needs wings, it needs someone with a sublime capacity for disregarding flat-footed commonsense if it is to get started at all. Talking of commonsense, what about our museums, our art galleries, our lending libraries? And for those who prefer to remain housebound the prolific flow of our radio and television programmes?

No prince in earlier times could command the range of music, drama, and discussion now produced for mass consumption. All that is needed is discrimination in the selection of programmes.

So why Centre 42? What does Wesker and those associated with him think they can do that is not already being done?

There is commonsense for you. But two things are left out . . . the loneliness and the destructive passivity of forever having things done to you, never yourself taking a direct hand in making them happen.

If Centre 42 did no more than stimulate more participation in the promotion and enjoyment of the arts, that in itself would be wholly worth while.

. . . When George Orwell wrote *Animal Farm* he was sick and dispirited. But he had something to say worth listening to. Arnold Wesker belongs to the same great company of originals. And he is neither sick nor dispirited. A forward thrust has got to come from somewhere. It would be that at a time when the calculations of the professional politicians and the still more professional calculations of the economists have manifestly failed to rescue us from the torpor of a subtly totalitarian culture, the only thing left is to give the poet his chance.[16]

Ossia Trilling[17] puts it far more simply. He believes that Wesker turned full-time to the management of Centre 42 because he fell into a "spiritual impasse" when he learned that the "proletarian public" for which he was writing was not coming to his plays.

ARNOLD WESKER

Wesker, however, is more far-seeing. "I would give anything," he writes, "to be able to convince myself that as an artist I can do no more than ply my craft and trust that the little ripples my pebble has caused will grow in ever-widening circles." [18] But— "I know that soon, along with my contemporaries, our work will be discarded as a fashion, having only been seen by a tiny portion of the population, no 'harm' will have been done and the remaining-fashion-conscious, elite public will be eager to devour the next sensation." [19]

III A Report

In the Centre 42 Annual Report 1961-1962,[20] Wesker explains in detail his commitment to Centre 42 and his views on the movement's achievements. From the date he became the artistic director of Centre 42 (November 26, 1961) to October, 1963, Centre 42 mounted six festivals of the arts. At this stage, Wesker felt free to say, "There is one important principle that I should like to hold against all argument: art is the right and need of every civilized community, as such it should be subsidized and not forced into paying for itself." [21] Rather triumphantly, he cries out, "Fortytwo [Centre 42, that is] works; this is a fact whatever our inadequacies may be." [22] Yet he cannot help adding, "If I say we have enemies I am not being wilfully dramatic; this is a discovery we have made in these last months and it must be acknowledged since it affects our future policy and approach." [23]

In his introduction to the Annual Report, Wesker touches not only on the crucial issues facing his movement, but on the problems facing British culture:

Our critics accuse us of dictating to an unwilling and otherwise perfectly happy community what should engage their emotional and intellectual sensibilities in the world of art. The popular phrase used is "taking culture to the masses"—this is a phrase which at once carries overtones of self-righteous soul saving, though God knows who these masses are or quite where they are to be found; our critics then assume, and this is where their thinking becomes irrational and emotional, that in wanting to broaden the frontiers of art we are implying that we are better people.

Apart from the assumption not being true, the attitude is one that does not make any sense. Far from assuming that all cultured people are better people, we know, only too well, that many are prigs and bores. Neither is the other assumption true that we are "taking culture to the masses"—it is a fact about our policy that we will go nowhere unless invited. That we stimulate a climate within which such invitations are made can hardly be construed as presumptuous; and to accuse us of dictating to an unwilling public, is to suggest we have no right mounting a festival for a community that invites us, thereby denying the artist his basic wish to share his creation with an audience.

Then we are "accused" of presuming to know what is good and bad in art—yet another example of illogical outrage. Surely inherent in any public enterprise is the right to create a standard, otherwise the function of all public performance must be questioned. It is not the right to create a cultural standard which should be denied but the need for a public to criticize which should be encouraged.[24]

Having replied to his critics in this fashion, Wesker now attacks the British intelligentsia and, logically, the Establishment:

A strange hysteria descends upon the English personality, especially the intelligentsia, when projects affecting "art and the people" are put into operation. There immediately springs to mind the image of patronizing salvationists wanting to do good. Over the years there has grown up such a tradition of meddling that now any public act, no matter how innocent or spontaneous the motive, is greeted with suspicion. Many artists and intellectuals are terrified of appearing to stand out beyond popular tastes for fear of seeming "square" or "not with it." For instance, serious discussions ensue concerning the relative merits of various pop singers and each of us frantically searches for a favorite pop star to applaud in order to remain "in touch." Against such a background of inverted snobbery a movement like Fortytwo is bound to appear presumptuous.

I think, therefore, we should stop the backward apologetic trend and acknowledge without shame that we are indeed presumptuous. That in fact we are presuming in human beings a marvellous complexity of sensibilities on all levels and rather than accept a narrow view of man's responses we shall act on the assumption that his potential for response is limitless. If this is called audacity then, good, we are audacious.

I believe that for many our real "crime" is that our work is conducted outside the commercial framework. It is this which makes us suspect; we are not making the arts available in the "legitimate" way. Our aim is not profit and, though not wishing here to discuss the merits of such a society, in a profit-motive society this places us in the realm of eccentricity, and eccentrics are irritating, embarrassing and disturbing. . . .[25]

Wesker, then, has connected Centre 42 with himself as an individual, as an Englishman who can contribute something to the culture of his time—and not necessarily or exclusively through the dramas he writes. "No wonder," he complains, "the artist is not really a respected person in society." He can be dispensed with because he "accepts the role of clown." [26]

But Wesker is no clown; he cannot be dispensed with; through Centre 42 he has established himself as a personality on the English scene. He is not merely a young man who writes plays for the edification of whatever public is willing to enter a theater to see his work. To him, the Word has special meaning and power. The theater is a battlefield. His people are, to him, not made-up characters, pallid inventions: they represent individuals, even when they have the weaknesses and the strengths of their class. Wesker believes he has significant things to say. If, for some reason, his messages cannot be communicated through his personal work, he hopes to be able to make a lasting impact through the movement of which he is the heart and soul.

CHAPTER 11

Wesker's Search for Identity

ARNOLD WESKER is a product of the British working class and he is a Jew. It is important that these factors be taken into account in any extended discussion of his work. Class distinction, less evident in the United States than in Great Britain, has special significance in England. The fact that Wesker, as a Jew, has emerged as an influential writer is by no means puzzling to American readers who have seen the Jewish writer break through impressively on the American literary scene.

I Man with a Cause

In his dramas, in articles, in essays, and in countless interviews, Wesker has expounded on the meaning of his work, on his goals and his dreams. In a conversation with Tom Milne,[1] Wesker, who talked about *Chips with Everything* prior to its presentation, said:

No one is going to like this play. There is a terrible truth, which is that people take what they want from a play. They are prepared to take it all, provided it is what they want. . . . I am tired of implication and subtlety. I hope that my alternative is not banality. I desperately want to be simple and direct. It seems to me that the simpler one can become, the less one leaves to the clever innuendo, the minute working out in detail—and the more honest one is being. This is probably what I mean when I say that I find art is not enough. I really would like to write a play which begins, "Once upon a time. . . ."

This is, of course, a wistful wish, for Wesker is a man with a cause. He does not write fairy tales, nor is he interested in the play of manners. He is committed to causes, as witness his leadership in the Centre 42 movement. He has been willing to give up the writing of dramas, at least temporarily, in order to promote Centre 42. Here he differs from John Osborne, who was an initial influence on his work. Yet Wesker has not copied Osborne, nor does he emulate Osborne's kind of anger. In Osborne's *Look Back in Anger,* Jimmy Porter makes a eloquent statement about causes:

I suppose people of our generation aren't able to die for good causes any longer. We had all that done for us, in the thirties and the forties, when we were still kids. There aren't any good, brave causes left. If the big bang does come, and we all get killed off, it won't be in aid of the old-fashioned, grand design. It'll just be for the Brave-New-nothing-very-much-thank-you. About as pointless and inglorious as stepping in front of a bus. No, there's nothing left for it, me boy, but to let yourself be butchered by the women.

Wesker, unlike Osborne, cares about important matters, and this is why critics like John Mander prefer Wesker's *Roots,* for example, to Osborne's *Look Back in Anger.*[2]

II *As a Jewish Writer*

As a Jewish writer, Wesker is something of a puzzle, for, while he has elected to depict Jewish characters on the stage, his Jews do not have depth as Jews, although Wesker himself is bothered by Jewish traits and attitudes. Here, too, he resembles many of the younger American-Jewish novelists, short story writers, and poets. Karl Shapiro, Philip Roth, Harvey Swados, Herbert Gold, Bruce Jay Friedman, and Norman Fruchter are notable Jewish writers who, like Wesker, are attracted to Jews and yet depict them as alienated, strange, neurotic people. Wesker, who comes from a different society, has chosen to make his Jews politically conscious rebels; yet his Jews are different from those drawn by English novelists like Frederic Raphael and Gerda Charles.

It should be realized that the Jewish writer in America has been more easily accepted by the Establishment than have the Jewish writers in England. Henry Popkin has reported that finally the English-Jewish writer has started his own tradition. This development is new. As long ago as 1917 Abraham Cahan published *The Rise of David Levinsky,* and the Jewish novel in America was born. It gave rise to a category of "Jewish fiction." When Israel Zangwill wrote his books about English Jews, he gained thousands of readers, but he did not start a trend. He was an original. His work was recognized, yet it was strange and alien on British soil. Jewish writers in England did not really start to emerge until after World War II.

Popkin writes that "Jewish writers of some distinction have appeared, and they have begun to assess themselves and their significance as Jews." [3] And he adds, "Some can be placed in reference to their American counterparts. Arnold Wesker has often, if inexactly, been hailed as a latter-day British equivalent to Clifford Odets; in his plays, he examines the problems of socialism more directly than Odets ever did, and he comments more affectionately, more nostalgically than Odets on the family ties that lie at the heart of Jewish life." [4]

In his analysis of playwrights Popkin concludes that "Wesker deals most directly with Jewish subjects, and with socialism and family life as necessary parts of the Jewish scene. His *Chicken Soup with Barley* shows a Jewish milieu warmed by the hope of socialism. In *Roots* we see a provincial Gentile family divided against itself and impervious to ideas. The daughter of the family, inspired by the socialist doctrine of her absent Jewish lover, loses the lover but—what is made to seem more important—keeps the socialism." [5]

Other Jewish critics have been discussing the "new Jewish wave" in England, some of them with more acuteness than others. Joseph Leftwich, a veteran Jewish translator, anthologist, and literary critic has made their series of observations:

The Mankowitz group had no sooner settled in than we suddenly got a new crop of young Jewish writers, mostly from the East End, including Arnold Wesker, Peter Shaffer, Harold Pinter and Bernard Kops. However, most of these seem more anxious to stress their alienation from the Jewish community than their connection with it. All the same, they can't get away from it. As Arnold Wesker has said of himself: "I feel a Jew, I am a Jew—there is no logic to it. Yet my roots though vague are real. And because I am a Jew I feel and write in a particular way." It is felt by the critics, who emphasize their Jewish rhythms of emotion and language. So much so that Allen Pryce-Jones feels that they "demand something which only Jewish actors can give."

Arnold Wesker has answered the question, "Why do I feel like a Jew?" by saying: "I feel a Jew because of the way my family spoke, because of the rhythms and patterns of their living"—even because of "the rituals I knew of, though I do not perform." [6]

The playwright himself has attempted to probe his own inner psyche on his Jewishness and has come up with murky, although interesting, responses. At a symposium on Jewish writing, writers, and "Jewishness," Wesker told his audience, in all candor, "You know, I suspect I am more Jewish than I think I am." He expanded on this observation by remarking, "I was not taught in a yeshiva, but one of my grandfathers was a shochet, and the other was a great rabbinical scholar, and I suppose their Jewish feeling must have been handed down to me subconsciously. At any rate, this shows in some of the imagery I use." [7]

III *The Problem of "Jewishness"*

"Jewishness" as such remains a problem with Wesker, and his bewilderment crops up at unexpected moments. In reviewing a book in *The Jewish Quarterly*, he made this side remark:

Kenneth Tynan said recently on a television programme that he considered that what the English theatre was lacking, and the American theatre had, was a great Jewish vitality. I feel a little guilty that this pleases me, but it does, and immediately there arises the question— "why?" All reason and logic about the "accident of birth" and the basic ingredients that make *all* men are of no avail; something Jewish in me responds to this observation and I submit to the muddled yet strong cry of the blood.

But what this response does not do, and here many Jews—artists in particular—are left wide open to attack and ridicule, is answer the question "what is a Jew?" And at a more concrete level, "why are not all conscious Jews in Israel?" One of the big frustrations I suffered during a recent trip to Israel was the feeling that I was a foreigner in that land—and nothing will resolve that! [8]

Gerda Charles, a novelist whose own work has crossed the Atlantic Ocean successfully, strongly suggests that Wesker's social consciousness is highly awakened precisely because he is Jewish. Here is her argument:

Why, for instance, has the work of Arnold Wesker made so tremendous an impression? Not, I think, though Wesker himself may deny this, because of the political content of his work but because he stresses that the most important good that can happen to any human being is an increased richness of personality. He sees (more clearly than any other contemporary writer) that, apart from those conditions which create brute poverty (which make a special case) the real deprivation in our social life is elsewhere; in starved characters, in stunted capacities for joy; in blindness to beauty and deafness to intelligence. Socialism, pure and simple, is not the answer to these kinds of malnutrition since though lack of education, lack of leisure, lack of energy can all to some extent be traced to lack of money this can't be wholly so. Indeed, when we consider our own Jewish past we see that there was probably more "reason for living" in many a *shtetel* in Eastern Europe in the last century with its interest in ideas, its ability to express them, its eagerness and respect for knowledge, than in the whole of many a London suburb today.

What Wesker is trying to do in his plays is to *wake us up*. He is telling us that we must learn to have opinions; opinions arrived at by open and flexible minds instead of obstinately held on to, lazy-minded cliches. He is telling us not to be afraid or suspicious or impatient with art—or for that matter with artists. He tells us we can all be artists in greater or lesser degree if we try. He has, in fact, the typically Jewish attitude that we must shop around for the best quality. . . . in living as well as carpeting. And above all he is telling us that we must learn to be articulate.[9]

American-Jewish writers are not as wedded to causes as Wesker. Too many of them deal almost exclusively with sexual relations, with romance, with love; they shy away from political and social issues. They are not trying to *wake us up*. Indeed, novelists like Herman Wouk, successful, skillful, and popular, defend middle-class virtues and pay little or no attention to political issues. And this statement is as true of Philip Roth as it is of Herman Wouk. It is not true of the contemporary English playwrights and novelists. Wesker, mulling over the Jewish influences in his work, wondering why he "responds to the cry of the blood," is as much a man of causes as he is an artist. There are those, of course, who call him a propagandist and deny him any artistry. One has to see his plays staged to be affected by them. Like O'Neill, he plays better than he reads. He is by no means certain about his ultimate views; he is still seeking, probing, wondering. This is not to be wondered at, for he is young; his world—and ours—is changing. He does not look at it from a distance, nor is he alienated from the social, economic, and political changes taking place. Perhaps his plays will, in time, become dated. He is, however, writing for his own time and apparently he has found his audience. He may still be searching for his identity—as Jew, as artist, as propagandist, as a seeker after causes. Meanwhile, he speaks for many while he looks inward to himself for himself.

CHAPTER 12

The Critical View

ARNOLD WESKER, when he was twenty-eight years of age, was asked by an interviewer,[1] "How important is fame to the dramatist?" Wesker conceded that it was important, but he preferred the word "respect" to "fame," for "respect" is a strong and valuable symbol of recognition. "It is important to a writer," Wesker continued, "to know that he is being listened to, that he is being understood, that he is being appreciated." [2] But Wesker understood the true meaning of the quesion, which he paraphrased as "How important is fame to Arnold Wesker?" [3] He answered his own query by saying, "I think I can promise one thing: I would not compromise on what I wanted to write for the sake of fame, or even for the sake of respect. If I did then I should soon be forgotten anyway, and probably lose the respect of the people from whom I most wanted it." [4]

This is a calmly stated view by a playwright who already had won acclaim for *The Kitchen, Chicken Soup with Barley,* and *Roots.* He had written *I'm Talking About Jerusalem* and his trilogy, the three plays about the Kahn family, would, later that year, be performed in a single season on a London stage. Wesker was, at this time, more than fairly confident that he had made his reputation. But a year before this interview, he had been less calm. He was irritated that some critics and directors had had enough of "working class" drama. Defending writers like himself —Kops, Delaney, and Behan—Wesker, in a letter to the *New Statesman,* was far more angry:

Here we are, having just started, most of us with only one play performed, we are just getting into our stride and beginning to learn about it all, and now some "fashion conscious" young smoothy comes along and declares with a bored yawn that "we've really had enough darling. . . ." We didn't set out to break down class barriers—no need to be frightened—we set out as artists and we haven't half started yet!

Now, listen to me, Mr. T. C. W. and Mr. G. D. and Mr. T. R., I've been writing for twelve years and it's only in the last year that I've been given my chance. I didn't write *Chicken Soup with Barley* simply because I wanted to amuse you with "working-class types" but because I saw my characters within the compass of a personal vision. I *have* a personal vision you know, and I will not be tolerated as a passing phase. You are going to see my next play soon, and I am going to write many more and you are going to see them as well, *not* because I'm a young *"primitive"* writer out on a leash for a bit of airing but because I'm a *good* writer with a voice of my own! [5]

I *He Seeks Respect*

This is an angry man talking, one who is aware that he, like others not of the Establishment, have had to fight their way forward. He may not have sought fame, but it has come. He wants respect and that, too, has come; but admiration certainly has not been wholehearted; and those few critics, mainly British, who have taken the trouble to write in some depth about Wesker have mixed praise with criticism. They do not fear him as a voice of rebellion. They do, however, question his skills, or his ideas. Curiously, I find that they too seldom credit him with the ability to create electricity in the theater itself—a quality too important to ignore. O'Neill, Shaw, and Williams have not always read well between the pages of a book. Somehow, when their characters have been placed on a stage, they—and the plays—have come to life. I am reminded of the glib criticisms of some popular novelists, like Maugham, of whom it has been said, "Well, yes, he's readable, but, after all, that's not enough." True, it isn't. But for a novelist to compel a reader to keep turning the pages to find out what is happening is no mean achievement. One is not necessarily a better novelist because he is a clumsy storyteller. By the same token, although a dramatist who brings life to the stage is not, by this accomplishment, a great dramatist, yet this gift does him no harm.

One British critic, Renee Winegarten,[6] concedes Wesker the passion and "vital impetus" of the Prophets and calls these great gifts. But, she asks, are they enough "to cover his glaring shortcomings in ideas and expression?" [7] Wesker blames the "inhuman, industrialist, capitalist society" [8] for too many of the human ills, according to Miss Winegarten. "Wesker," she writes, "takes no account of the complexity and corruption of human nature, its convolutions, its hidden abysses. He does not face the fact that human beings, regardless of birth and class, are a tissue of incoherence and inconsistency." [9] This is, I feel, a misreading of Wesker and his plays. He *does* take account of the complexity of human nature, especially in *Chicken Soup with Barley,* and in the character of Beatie Bryant in *Roots.* Pip Thompson in *Chips with Everything* is not a simple character, and, in the speech by the Pilot Officer in the same play, corruption is rather clearly understood, especially by the playwright. Miss Winegarten also makes this charge against Wesker: "He has not invented characters whom he ceases to manipulate." [10] This may sound, at first, like a profound statement. It is, on reflection, a silly one. Every playwright invents characters and manipulates them. If he doesn't, he is undisciplined and has no idea of what he is trying to say or do.

Roger Gellert, another English critic, generally admires Wesker but wishes he did less propagandizing. "I can't help feeling," he informs us, "that the proselytizing tendency is Wesker's biggest pitfall as a dramatist." [11] But, when one reads Gellert more closely, one senses that the two men—the critic and the playwright—differ only slightly, really. Gellert says that Wesker "sees Culture almost in a bacteriological sense, as a benign germ that is bound to spread if let loose in a crowd. My own view would be that this germ can only enter slyly, often through the wounds inflicted by life, whereas its deliberate injection into healthy philistine organisms does nothing but rouse jeering antibodies." [12] Both men, in brief, are on the same side; they disagree only about how culture should be injected. They both believe that it is lacking, and so, in a sense, they are on the same side; thus Gellert admires *Chips with Everything* as a demonstration that Wesker is showing a "growing virtuosity." [13]

The noted critic, V. S. Pritchett, who has his qualifications about Wesker, recognizes in him a strong force in the British theater. He considers *The Kitchen* to be the best of Wesker's plays (a minority opinion) because it is the best theater, even if less ambitious than the others. When this article was written, *Chips with*

Everything had not yet been produced, and Pritchett had not seen *I'm Talking About Jerusalem* on the stage. *The Kitchen,* according to Pritchett, "has a virtuosity and a force which recall O'Casey, O'Neill and moments of Gorki." [14] Pritchett finds the Trilogy uneven. *Chicken Soup with Barley* does not have the storytelling power of *The Kitchen* and has the same "journalistic commentary" [15] which, for Pritchett, ruins *I'm Talking About Jerusalem. Roots,* to him, is a sound play which would have benefited by cutting: "All it has to say is in the last act. . . ." [16] And he is warm in his praise for the high theatricality and honesty of Beatie Bryant's final speech: "This is one of Wesker's best moments. It is splendid theatre; no novelising here. He has shown great art in the delicate job of showing ideas growing in minds not equipped, apparently, to contain them." [17]

John Rosselli, writing from London for *The Reporter* in New York, at a time when *Chips with Everything* had opened in London with great success, reiterates the complaints and criticisms of those who find Wesker "posterlike" and propagandistic. He writes that Wesker's "imaginative understanding does reach as far as the struggle of young English people to speak freely with their contemporaries." [18] But he makes another valid point, which too few critics have noticed or noted:

Wesker's gift, in fact, is for the side of the theater that has most to do with dance. One of the best moments in *Roots* comes when the farm girl does an awkward little dance in an attempt to show her mother what she feels on hearing Mendelssohn's Fourth Symphony. In *The Kitchen* the exasperated cooks and waitresses build up to a sort of lunch-hour ballet. His other plays, even at their crudest, are full of strong stage pictures. In *Chips* one of the best scenes—thanks partly to the director John Dexter, who has put on all of Wesker's plays—is the wordless, nimble raid on the coal supply; another is the incompetent Smiler's running on one spot as he tries to flee from his tormentors. The drill movements too are dances of a kind; the play is punctuated with moments of song and collective movement.[19]

Rosselli, then, sees Wesker's plays as staged works: He is aware of their impact when seen. This aspect is too frequently overlooked, because Wesker is so eager to make his message understood. But he never forgets that he is a dramatist first. And he is.

II *Recognition of Achievement*

A. R. Jones recognizes in the Trilogy a work of enormous achievement, and he writes of it in Wesker's own terms; that is, he attempts to explain what Wesker is trying to *say*. Jones sees the people in the Kahn family as people, not as puppets. He appreciates Wesker's concern for human beings and declares that Wesker has virtues which stem from two main sources: "Firstly, from the way in which his passionate concern for individuals transforms what otherwise might have been puppet figures into people of life and substance about whom we too are intensely concerned; and, secondly, from the severe and often terrifying honesty with which he pursues his theme, without compromise or favour, without permitting his ideals to subvert his material or his politics to tempt him to easy or clear-cut decisions." [20]

Unlike those critics who disagree with Wesker because they view life from another side of society, Jones relates Wesker's Trilogy to all of contemporary life and thereby sees it as a major achievement of our time and as a reason for our faith in the drama rather than in the novel of our day. Here is Jones at his best:

In this trilogy Wesker has rewritten the myth of our time and re-written it from the point of view of those who suffered and, somehow, survived the crises and disillusionments of the last twenty-five years. It is not the conventional myth manufactured by the political dream factories but a profoundly moving embodiment in imaginative terms of his generation's experience of the history of our time. His view of the jaded themes of society and humanity carries conviction by virtue of its freshness and spontaneity and by the same token of freshness these themes are renewed. People really matter to Wesker; he is passionately concerned about the weak and the strong and the indifferent. . . .

Wesker's plays are full of incident and dramatic interest, however domestic. His world is one of the family, an intimate group bound by affection and experience; moving through social changes and being changed by them. He is sometimes clumsy with inexperience, unable quite to handle the sheer wealth that his themes throw up; his characters are not altogether clearly conceived or fully projected and his dramatic situations are often over-contrived to the point where the theatrical machinery creaks. He has not yet learnt to handle direct conflict and his trilogy has a certain ingrown quality the potential of which is not entirely brought out in dramatic terms. But to say that

he is promising would be insulting; the trilogy represents a real achievement. Wesker and his contemporaries have taken the initiative in
drama, and the life of the theatre might well compensate us for the
death of, say, the novel as an art form.[21]

In the United States little has been written about Wesker's total
body of work. *Chips with Everything* was widely reviewed, as has
been indicated in the chapter devoted to that drama; *Roots* was
noticed more or less casually in the American press. Following the
opening of *Chips with Everything* in New York, *The New York
Times Magazine* published a Sunday feature on Wesker by John
Beavan, under the title of "Missionary in the Theatre." [22] Wesker
came to New York for the opening of *Chips with Everything*, and
soon local newspapers and television stations interviewed him and
discussed, mostly, *Chips with Everything* and the Centre 42
movement. Wesker had become something of a "celebrity." Yes,
he told his interviewers, he was interested in a national theater
movement in England, and he was seeking funds to maintain and
expand such a movement. Yes, he was writing another play. He
returned to England with *Chips with Everything* running strongly
and his own reputation sufficiently enhanced for his New York
producer[23] to announce that *The Kitchen* would eventually be
brought to Broadway.

It should not be overlooked that Wesker's work has gone far
beyond England and the United States. Foreign rights to *Chicken
Soup with Barley* have been sold in Italy[24] and Germany. *Roots*
has been sold to publishing and producing interests in France,
Germany, Holland, the Scandinavian countries, Argentina,
Czechoslovakia, Brazil, and Turkey. *I'm Talking About Jerusalem*
also has been bought—theatrical and publishing rights—in Germany, Yugoslavia, and the Scandinavian countries. *The Kitchen's*
foreign rights were purchased in France, Japan, Germany, Holland, Italy, and Argentina. And *Chips with Everything* has been
purchased in Belgium, Germany, Holland, Scandinavia, and Argentina.[25]

More and more, books on the drama include chapters on Wesker, and John Russell Taylor's volume already has been updated
to include *Chips with Everything*.[26] Wesker's name appears, in
passing, in reviews and articles devoted not so much to his own

[118]

work as to the contemporary theater. Together with Pinter and Osborne, he is one of Great Britain's "Big Three," although others are crowding in and promising to increase the number of lively British dramatists.

III *An Interesting Playwright*

One must constantly bear in mind that Wesker is in the midst of his creativity. He has talked about a play on Jesus. He has worked on—and put aside—a musical. After *Chips with Everything* was offered on the American stage, Wesker returned to London and, in the period of one year, wrote two new plays, *Their Very Own and Golden City* and *The Four Seasons*. He is always busy with one script or another,[27] while working hard to keep Centre 42 alive and developing. He is constantly available to the press and to other media of communications, for he is the heart of a theatrical movement as well as a practicing playwright. Certainly, he has been both belittled and overpraised. *The Kitchen* is not so good as O'Casey's work, and *Roots* is not the finest play of the century. Time will eventually place Wesker in better perspective. There is no doubt at all, however, that he is one of the most interesting playwrights in the world today. He is prolific; he keeps writing. He is not apathetic, nor is he writing by rote. Many of the leading American dramatists are drained and no longer have any imagination. Wesker is still under compulsion to write, for he still has much to say. And when he says it, he doesn't need psychiatrists to explain his work, as a handful of America's leading playwrights do.

Some critics have wondered in what direction his work will turn. Others feel that he has not yet written purely from the imagination, that he has continued to draw exclusively from autobiographical sources. Still other critics have expressed the fear that Wesker will continue to repeat himself, because he has been didactic in his plays and has been hammering home the single-minded message that the working man has the ability to wake up and change his society.

These critics have not yet read or seen Wesker's two latest dramas. Quite apart from their dramatic success or failure, they are—thematically—somewhat different from Wesker's earlier work. *Their Very Own and Golden City* is, of course, political, but is more ambitious than anything else Wesker ever attempted. *The Four Seasons,* unlike the other new play, is very narrow in scope, with only two characters. *Chips with Everything* was different from the Wesker Trilogy, and every new play is unlike its predecessor.

The chances remain excellent that Wesker will grow and improve on his already impressive body of work. The climate in Great Britain encourages writers like Wesker. More and more, the modern novel and drama in England reflect the ferment in British society. Alan Sillitoe, David Storey, John Wain, John Braine, and women like Doris Lessing and Shelagh Delaney represent the new writer, the writer with a strong desire to depict life in England that is not the life of the upper classes, but that of the working man.

IV *A Committed Artist*

Arnold Wesker, like those just mentioned, is a committed writer. He is aware that politics is part of man's life. He is not afraid to deal with—and judge—political movements. He is prepared to castigate, attack, and ask for improvements in the world and in Britain. In a thoughtful essay[28] Wesker has pointed out that art is serious, and is not a "hobby." The people of England, he insists, need not look to art to "fill in" their increasingly large number of leisure hours. Wesker is still on the attack when he writes:

To associate the need for art with the increase of leisure is false; the difference is a real and important one because it affects our approach. You don't read books, go to theatres or listen to music because you're bored or because there's nothing better to do—this reduces art to being a mere makeshift. You read books out of a burning human need to share another man's thoughts and experience, out of a compelling curiosity for the story he has to tell; you listen to music because without it your spirit must dry and shrivel; music is a release, a stimulant, a need—like a blast of fresh air—not a mere noise to fill the silence between bored bites of food.[29]

In reply to a question raised by some of Wesker's observations in this essay, the playwright shows again his strong feeling for the "message" of the artist. His commitment is complete. Here is his conception of the role of the arts, and note that he does not hesitate to be radical when he feels that radicalism is called for to carry forward his concepts:

The arts . . . are the means through which men are given the chance —slender though it may be—to understand the marvellous nature and complexity of their lives. This is a fact, it is the artist who has inspired the politician, the poet who has guided the thoughts of philosophers, the architect who has shaped the patterns of man's daily life. But the arts are a language with basic rules and principles which need to be learned, and yet our educational system provides no teachers of that language. No cultural programme and certainly no ministry of culture stands the slightest chance of succeeding unless there is a radical change in the educational system which brings the arts on to the same level of importance as mathematics. Art Masters and teachers of English literature do not answer this problem. Neither do I talk about lessons in schools on the "appreciation of the arts." I'm talking about the need to acknowledge that the artist's work is a battlefield where ideas are fought and values affirmed.[30]

Wesker is willing to move onto the battlefield for his ideas. He may not be a prophet, but he is not bothered that some accuse him of donning the mantle of a prophet. Perhaps to Americans— who are more affluent than their neighbors, who have lived through their own Depression, who have been cynical about politicians—Wesker is "old-fashioned." But old fashions have a habit of becoming once again new fashions. The world is restless and in constant flux. There is more to art than concentrating and focusing on love affairs and sexual conflicts. The world is large and man's activities are many. Wesker has broadened horizons and always has remembered to create plays that have social passion. Now his dramas are being performed all over the world. Obviously Wesker's work is not narrow in its interests or parochial, even when he is depicting a Jewish family in London, or an inarticulate girl seeking to express herself among her own people living on a farm in Norfolk; or the rise and corruption of a Labour leader, or the lack of communication between a pair of lovers.

Arnold Wesker's achievement has been considerable. His latest work is more experimental, more ambitious, and digs deeper than his earlier, more conventional plays. One looks forward to his future work with honest anticipation, for he is a lively, thinking dramatist—one who speaks for an entire generation.

Notes and References

Preface

1. Taylor. *The Angry Theatre* (New York, 1962), p.143.
2. He was born on May 24, 1932, in London.
3. It opened at the Mayfair Theatre on March 6, 1961.
4. In an interview with the author in New York City on September 30, 1963, during Wesker's first visit to the United States, prior to the opening of *Chips with Everything* at the Plymouth Theatre on October 1, 1963.
5. In a talk with Wesker on October 3, 1963, the day after I saw the New York production.
6. Wesker to the author in the September 30th interview.
7. Even before Wesker's attack on the Establishment in *Chips with Everything,* British critics were stressing his similarities to Osborne—often however, giving the preference to Wesker. John Mander, in *The Writer and Commitment* (Philadelphia, 1962), wrote on page 188: "To say that the arrival of *Roots,* three years after the first night of *Look Back in Anger* in May 1956, must alter our judgment of the latter play is not to say merely that Mr. Wesker has learned from Mr. Osborne's mistakes and contrived to do it better. My assumption is that both Mr. Osborne and Mr. Wesker start out with much the same ideology ('If you don't care, you'll die'), but that what emerges from the plays is something radically different. My argument is that *Roots* achieves what *Look Back in Anger* might have achieved, but in fact only promises."
8. Taylor, *The Angry Theatre.*
9. Others include novelist and playwright Wolf Mankowitz; playwrights Harold Pinter, Bernard Kops, Peter Shaffer, and Lionel Bart; novelists Gerda Charles, Brian Glanville, Frederic Raphael, and Alexander Baron; and critics Bernard Levin and Charles Marowitz. Kops, in *The World is a Wedding* (New York, 1963), has written an autobiography in which he stresses his Jewish background.

[123]

Chapter One

1. John Russell Taylor in *Anger and After* (Harmondsworth, Middlesex, Penguin Books, 1963; a volume which also appeared in the United States in a Penguin paperback [a Pelican book], Baltimore, 1963, and in a trade edition under the title of *The Angry Theatre. New British Drama* [New York, 1962]). Irving Wardle, "Revolt Against the West End," *Horizon* (January, 1963), and Irving Wardle, "New Waves on the British Stage," *The Twentieth Century* (London, Summer, 1963), reprinted in *Plays and Players* (London, October, 1963), pp. 12-14. Laurence Kitchin, *Mid-Century Drama* (London, 1960).

2. A number of interesting references to the British films, and their relationship to English dramatists have been made in various issues of *The Transatlantic Review*, in which noted film and stage directors were interviewed. Of special interest are these: "Conversations at the Royal Court Theatre with Tony Richardson and Lindsay Anderson," by Robert Rubens (Spring, 1962), pp. 5-18; and "An interview with Alan Schneider," by Jean-Claude Van Itallie (Summer, 1962), pp. 12-23. Richardson, Anderson, and Schneider are illuminating when they talk about their problems as film and stage producers and directors. Schneider, in particular, who has staged Pinter, Brecht, Albee, and Williams, has some valuable insights into Wesker and Osborne.

3. Taylor, *Anger and After*, p. 13.

4. *Ibid.*, p. 14.

5. Quoted in *Anger and After*, p. 31.

6. Much of the biographical material in this chapter, as well as this quotation, is drawn from "Arnold Wesker," in *Current Biography* (February, 1962), pp. 43-45.

7. Quoted from an interview with Laurence Kitchin in *Mid-Century Drama*, p. 216.

Chapter Two

1. Wesker, *The Kitchen* (New York, 1961), p. 5.

2. *Ibid.*

3. Jill Pomerance, who interviewed Wesker in his home, and published the interview in *New Theatre Magazine* (April, 1960), published by the Green Room Society of the Drama Department of the University of Bristol.

4. In the same interview.

5. Taylor, *Anger and After*, p. 143.

6. *Ibid.*, p. 144.

7. This statement was made to me, after Wesker had seen my treat‑ment of Taylor's remark.

8. Taylor, *Anger and After.*

9. In an article entitled "Arnold Wesker," in the London *Times* (December 12, 1963), signed "From Our Special Correspondent," but written by John Russell Taylor. Mr. Taylor sent me this article, which contains an interview with Wesker.

Chapter Three

1. The program is, of course, unpaginated. I picked it up in 1960 in London, where I saw *Roots*, with Joan Plowright as Beatie.

2. In the same program, which states that the Wesker Trilogy is presented by the English Stage Company by arrangement with the Belgrade Theatre, Coventry.

3. From the program.

4. Also from the program.

5. *Chicken Soup with Barley*, in *New English Dramatists* 1, three plays introduced and edited by E. Martin Browne (Harmondsworth, Middlesex, Penguin Books, 1959).

6. This factor is of no importance in *I'm Talking About Jerusalem*, but it is a curious omission, for it plays a fairly significant part in establishing Dave's character in *Chicken Soup with Barley*.

7. The critics differ on which of the three plays is the most effective and the best theater. Many feel that *Chicken Soup with Barley* is the best made of the three dramas, which is odd, considering it was one of Wesker's earliest efforts. However, *Chips with Everything*, which is not part of the Wesker Trilogy, currently ranks as his finest achieve‑ment.

8. American playwrights rarely inject politics into their plays, and surely we have had very few dramas in which the heroes are Com‑munists and in which a major spokesman takes pride in the fact that a Communist sits in the House of Commons (or, in this country, in Con‑gress).

9. In my chapter on *I'm Talking About Jerusalem* I point out the real-life character on whom Dave is based. His name is Ralph Saltiel and I served in the United States Air Force on the island of Ceylon with him, when he was in the Royal Air Force. Ada's views expressed here were expressed to me by Ralph Saltiel and I recall that he wrote to his wife Della (the Ada of the play) on this very subject, more or less along the same lines.

10. Oddly, this struggle to maintain a Jewish identity is not referred to anywhere in the text of *I'm Talking About Jerusalem*, although Wes‑

ker himself, in interviews, essays, and lectures, has indicated his interest in Jewish issues. This subject is treated in the chapter entitled "Wesker's Search for Identity."

11. A weakness of *The Kitchen* is that it is impersonal. Ronnie, in *Chicken Soup with Barley*, conveys his bitterness in a few words, while the reader, or spectator, finds it difficult to identify with any of the men or women in *The Kitchen*.

Chapter Four

1. *Roots*, Penguin Books (Harmondsworth, Middlesex, 1959).

2. Wesker himself worked in a hotel kitchen, and his wife was a waitress before they married.

3. *Roots*.

4. Dexter, "Working with Arnold," in *Plays and Players* (London: April 1962), p. 11.

5. Quotations from some of the more important reviews will be found in the bibliography.

6. Hatch, *Horizon* (July, 1961), pp. 116-18. In *The Nation* of March 25, 1961, p. 272, Hatch has spelled out his views in a somewhat different fashion: "Wesker's people are rootless in the sense that they have been cut off where they stand, their traditions atrophied beneath them and their lives rotting. . . ." If the American production were more English," Hatch says, it would be easier to understand, but this is an American project in cast and direction. It feels like O'Neill with assistance from Odets, assuming that both had abruptly lost contact with their sources. Because of this ambivalence of milieu, the audience falls back on the theater itself as the only place where the events occur. The play becomes 'realism' rather than real; that is always embarrassing, the more so here because *Roots* is so frankly hortatory. Wesker is a dramatist of formidable technical skill, which is not today so very rare. But he is using it in an effort to split a way into the monolithic inferiority of his times, and that today is so rare in the theatre as to evoke wonder and gratitude."

7. *Ibid.*

8. Hartley, *A State of England* (New York, 1963), p. 186.

9. *Ibid.*, p.187.

10. *Ibid.*

11. Findlater, "Plays and Politics," *The Twentieth Century* (London: September, 1960), pp. 235-41.

12. Kitchin, *Mid-Century Drama* (London, 1960), p. 113.

13. *Ibid.*

14. Taylor, *Anger and After*, Penguin Books. (Harmondsworth,

Middlesex, 1963). This is the paperback title of *The Angry Theatre*. In this revised edition, which includes a lengthy study of Wesker and *Chips with Everything* as well as an analysis of the revised *The Kitchen,* Taylor reports on *Roots:* "When it opened in Coventry the notices were decidedly mixed, the only point of general agreement being the brilliance of Joan Plowright's performance in the central role. But by the time the play reached London word had somehow got round that it offered a great theatrical experience, and so this time the notices were almost unanimously favourable. It is, admittedly, always difficult to disentangle the merits of a performance from those of the play performed, but in retrospect one cannot help wondering how far the critics were swayed in their judgment by the superb performance of Joan Plowright as Beatie; later productions with other actresses have tended noticeably to cut the play down to size. . . ."

15. Mander, *The Writer and Commitment* (Philadelphia, 1962) pp. 196-98.

16. *Ibid.*

17. *Ibid.*, p. 209.

18. *Ibid.*

19. *Ibid.*, p. 210.

Chapter Five

1. Taylor, *Anger and After.* Penguin Books. (Harmondsworth, Middlesex, 1963), p. 140.

2. Muller, *I'm Talking About Jerusalem.* Penguin Books. (Harmondsworth, Middlesex, 1960), p. 8.

3. *Ibid.*, p. 7.

4. Gindin, "Anger as Affirmation," *Postwar British Fiction* (University of California Press, 1962), pp. 84-85.

5. Taylor, *Anger and After*, p. 142.

6. Dexter, "Working with Arnold," *Plays and Players* (London: April, 1962), p. 11.

Chapter Six

1. Quoted on the jacket of the American edition of *Chips with Everything* (New York, 1962).

2. Wesker, "Art Is Not Enough," *The Twentieth Century* (London: February, 1961) pp. 191-94. In a conversation with Tom Milne. This specific quotation is on page 192.

3. Ibid. pp. 192-93.

4. Dexter, "Chips and Devotion," *Plays and Players* (London: December, 1962), p. 32.

5. *Ibid.*

6. Tynan, "The Chip and the Shoulder," *The Observer* (London: May 6, 1962).

7. Trilling, "The New English Realism," *Tulane Drama Review* (Winter, 1962), p. 185.

8. Tynan, "The Chip and the Shoulder."

9. *Ibid.*

10. Amis, "Not Talking About Jerusalem," *The Spectator* (London: August 10, 1962), p. 190. In this book review of *Chips with Everything* and *The Wesker Trilogy*. Amis makes clear that he is judging Wesker on the published work. He hasn't bothered to see any of Wesker's plays in England!

11. *Ibid.*

12. *Ibid.*

13. *Ibid.*

14. *Ibid.*

15. Gascoigne, "Goodbye, Mr. Chips," *The Spectator* (London: May 11, 1962), p. 621.

16. *Ibid.*

17. *Ibid.*

18. *Ibid.*

19. *Ibid.*

20. McGuiness, "Culture with Chips," *The London Magazine* (London: July, 1962), p. 48.

21. *Ibid.*

22. *Ibid.*, p. 49.

23. Wesker, quoted from an article in the *Transatlantic Review*. Reprinted in John Russell Taylor's *Anger and After*. Penguin Books (Harmondsworth, Middlesex: 1963), p. 146.

24. Taylor, *Anger and After,* pp. 148-49.

25. *The Jewish Quarterly* (London: Autumn, 1962).

26. Mark Cohen, "Impersonal Hero."

27. *Ibid.*, p. 49.

28. "Chips with Everything," *Queen* (London: May 15, 1962), p. 11.

29. *Ibid.*

30. August, 1962.

31. Dennis, "What Though the Field Be Lost," *Encounter* (London: August, 1962), p. 44.

32. *Ibid.*

33. *Ibid,* p. 45.

34. *Kerr,* "Magic Over Matter," *New York,* The Sunday *Herald Tribune Magazine* (October 27, 1963), p. 25.

35. *Ibid.*

36. Kerr, "Chips with Everything," *New York Herald Tribune* (October 2, 1963), p. 18.

37. Taubman, "Life with R.A.F. Trainees," *New York Times* (October 2, 1963), p. 49.

38. Hewes, "Keep the Home Fires Frying," *Saturday Review* (October 19, 1963), p. 30.

39. *Ibid.*

40. Lewis, "Chips with Everything," *Cue* (October 12, 1963), p. 15.

41. *Ibid.*

42. Clurman, "Theatre," *The Nation* (October 26, 1963), pp. 267-68.

43. "A Fine Dish," *Newsweek* (October 14, 1963), p. 72.

44. "Sheep That Don't Say Baa," *Time* (October 11, 1963), p. 72.

45. Brustein, "The Backwards Birds," *The New Republic* (October 19, 1963). In a review of both Osborne's *Luther* and Wesker's *Chips with Everything.*

46. Popkin, "Class War with Everything," *The New Leader* (October 28, 1963), p. 31.

47. It seems that, whenever politics on the American stage is discussed, Clifford Odets comes to the mind of most of our critics. Throughout the reviews of Wesker's work, Odets is mentioned again and again as a standard of comparison, although they are decades apart in their work. Moreover, Wesker genuinely writes of politics in *Chicken Soup with Barley;* Odets concentrates a great deal more on his people than on any ideas they may have.

48. Sigal, *"Chips with Everything."*

Chapter Seven

1. At this writing, *Their Very Own and Golden City* has not yet been staged anywhere, although in a letter to me (December 17, 1964) Wesker wrote that the drama "won first prize in the Italian Premio Marzotto competition. This competition is held yearly and established European playwrights are invited to submit works that have not yet been performed. The jury consisted of people like Jean Vilar, Katina Paxinou, Martin Esslin, Jacques Huisman and others." In this letter Wesker also disclosed that he was having difficulty in finding an experienced director and had settled on "a young director."

2. Instead of a dedication to this play, Wesker quotes two long and pertinent paragraphs from the work of William Morris (1834-96) which are prophetic and immediately set the tone for *Their Very Own and Golden City.* Here are the paragraphs:

". . . and accordingly the Trade Unionists and their leaders who

were once the butt of the most virulent abuse from the whole of the
Upper and Middle classes are now praised and petted by them because they do tacitly or openly acknowledge the necessity for the
master's existence; it is felt that they are no longer the enemy; the
class struggle in England is entering into a new phase, which may even
make the once dreaded Trade Unions allies of capital, since they in
their turn form a kind of privileged group among the workmen; in
fact they now no longer represent the whole class of workers as working *men* but rather as charged with the office of keeping the human
part of the capitalists' machinery in good working order and freeing
it from any grit of discontent.

"Now that's the blind alley which the Trade Unions have now got
into; I say again if they are determined to have masters to manage
their affairs, they must expect in turn to pay for that luxury . . . remembering that the price they pay for their so-called captains of indus-
try is no mere money payment—no mere tribute which once paid
leaves them free to do as they please but an authoritative ordering of
the whole tenor of their lives, what they shall eat, drink, wear, what
houses they shall have, books, or newspapers rather, they shall read,
down to the very days on which they shall take their holidays like a
drove of cattle driven out from the stable to grass."

3. It is interesting that Dobson, the journalist, appears in Wesker's
I'm Talking About Jerusalem. There Dobson is a former socialist, now
a cynical businessman, who argues that Dave, in carrying forward
his own ideas to their logical conclusion, can help create chaos in our
contemporary society.

4. Wesker seems to fall into a trap of using naive images and, at
first, one is embarrassed for him. But through repetition—or sincerity—
or a blend of the two—he makes us accept his words.

Chapter Eight

1. The only political note struck in the play is sounded in the dedication, which, obviously, cannot appear on stage. The dedication is
worth reproducing here because it reveals Wesker's political views,
and is effective writing:

to

the romantic revolution

to

Maria Rosa, Edmundo, Abelardo, Bertina

to

the innocent revolution

to

Fidel, Camilo, Che, Pepe

to
the undergraduate revolutionaries
to
Ingrid, Jose, Rebecca, Ugo
to
the amateur administrators
to
Mario, Calvert, Maria Elena, Fernando
to
the soldiers who sing
and the singers who guard
to
Portocarrero, Milian, George, Chiki
to
the sea by my window, the Sierra Maestra
the Varadero beach and the peso that is not worth a dollar
to
the glorious mess you've made for
the children who read and the waiters who learn
to Haydee Santamaria, Miriam, Pablo, Teresa

not because of the slogans which soon no one will believe
but because you've turned the barracks to schools

not because of the traitors you've killed to the whine of righteous words
but because of the seeds of forgiveness I know you have

not because you would ever win if the big fight came
but because you are not afraid that you might lose

to Cuba.

2. In a note at the end of the play Wesker, who had been a pastry cook, describes in professional detail precisely how to make apple strudel. Then, in the only humor displayed in the manuscript, he adds the following: "None of this preparation is done in the play. The paste and ingredients are ready in time for the scene. Only the pulling and filling are acted." And in a final line: "Advice should be sought from a high class pastry cook."

Chapter Nine

1. *The Jewish Quarterly* (London: Winter, 1958-59), pp. 32-42. Reprinted in *Caravan: A Jewish Quarterly Omnibus,* edited by Jacob Sonntag (New York and London, 1962), pp. 160-84.

2. The full text of this original television play, presented by BBC Television on December 8, 1963, was sent to me by Arnold Wesker. Following rehearsals beginning on October 28, 1963, it was first recorded for the "First Night Series" on November 17, 1963. The first version, with fewer scenes and minus the concluding one, was published in *The Jewish Quarterly,* under the title *The Menace,* in the Spring, 1963, issue.

3. Laurence Kitchin, *Mid-Century Drama.* (London, 1960), p. 217.

4. Quoted from a memorandum, dated May 12, 1964, from Wesker to the author.

5. Taylor, "Mr. Wesker's 'Menace,'" *The Listener* (London: December 12, 1963), p. 1001.

6. *Ibid.*

Chapter Ten

1. Kops, "The Young Writer and the Theatre," *The Jewish Quarterly* (London: Summer, 1961), p. 19.

2. *Ibid.*

3. Wesker, "The Secret Reins," *Encounter* (London: March, 1962), p. 4.

4. Marowitz, "Oh Mother, Is It Worth It?", *Theatre Arts* (May, 1962), p. 21.

5. *Centre 42, First Stage in a Cultural Revolution* (London, 1962), unpaginated, and *Annual Report 1961-1962 Fortytwo.* Both published by Centre 42 Limited, 20 Fitzroy Square, London.

6. *Centre 42, First Stage in a Cultural Revolution.*

7. Marowitz, "Oh Mother, Is It Worth It?"

8. *Centre 42.*

9. Wesker, "The Secret Reins," p. 6.

10. *Ibid.*

11. Marowitz, "Oh Mother, Is It Worth It?", p. 22.

12. *Ibid.*

13. *Ibid.,* p. 72.

14. The *Centre 42* brochure and the *Annual Report,* both of which outline the plans for the movement, also list the men and women who have assumed responsibility for the organization, which has been incorporated as a Company and is a National Charity registered under the Charities Act, 1960. In the Annual Report it is stated that Centre

Notes and References

42, in 1962, was granted £10,000 "from the Calouste Gulbenkian Foundation to cover the cost of administration for two years." The list of officers of Centre 42 was slightly different in *Centre 42* and in the *Annual Report*.

According to the *Annual Report,* which is the more recent publication, Arnold Wesker is the Director, Beba Lavrin is Assistant Director, Michael Henshaw is Secretary, and Olive Barker is Festival Organizer. The Council of Management included the following individuals: Olive Barker, Ralph Bond, Sir William Carron, Frank Cousins, Michael Croft, Clive Goodwin, Michael Henshaw, Ted Hill, Ted Kotcheff, Michael Kustow, Beba Lavrin, Jennie Lee M.P., Tom Maschler, Jeremy Sandford, Keith Turner, Frank Ward, and Arnold Wesker. Missing from the list of the earlier brochure are Doris Lessing and Alun Owen among others.

Sponsors, or Friends of Centre 42, are: Countess Albemarle, Malcom Arnold, Dame Peggy Ashcroft, Stanley Baker, Mark Bass, Percy Belcher, John Berger, Sidney Bernstein, Robert Bolt, R. W. Briginshaw, Edward Carter, Michael Citroen, Cyril Cooper, the Bishop of Coventry, Johnny Dankworth, George Devine, Maurice Essex, Gerald Gardiner QC, Graham Greene, Milton Grundy, Lord Harewood, Arnold Haskell, Cecile Hemans, Barbara Hepworth, Harold Hobson, Richard Hoggart, Jack Hylton, Pamela Hansford Johnson, Cleo Laine, Harold Lever M.P., Sir Compton Mackenzie, Richard Marsh M.P., Tom Maschler, Peggy Middleton, Spike Milligan, Baron Moss, Eric Newton, Sir Laurence Olivier, John Piper, Joan Plowright, J. B. Priestley, George Rapp, Terence Rattigan, Sir Herbert Read, Vanessa Redgrave, Sir John Rothenstein, Nicholas Sekers, Peter Sellers, Barnett Shine, Alan Sillitoe, C. P. Snow, Feliks Topolski, Kenneth Tynan, Lord Walston, and Raymond Williams.

15. Lee, "Wesker's Centre 42," *Encounter* (London: August, 1962), pp. 95-96.

16. *Ibid.*

17. Trilling, "The New English Realism," *Tulane Drama Review* (Winter, 1962), pp. 185-86.

18. Wesker, "The Secret Reins," p. 4.

19. *Ibid.*

20. *Annual Report 1961-1962 Fortytwo,* pp. 2-5.

21. *Ibid.*

22. *Ibid.*

23. *Ibid.,* p. 2.

24. *Ibid.,* p. 3.

25. *Ibid.*

26. Wesker, "The Secret Reins," p. 6.

[133]

Chapter Eleven

1. Arnold Wesker in "Art Is Not Enough," a conversation with Tom Milne, *The Twentieth Century* (London: February, 1961), pp. 190-94.

2. Mander, *The Writer and Commitment* (Philadelphia, 1962), p. 188: "To say that the arrival of *Roots*, three years after the first night of *Look Back In Anger* in May 1956, must alter our judgment of the latter play is not to say merely that Mr. Wesker has learned from Mr. Osborne's mistakes and contrived to do it better. My assumption is that both Mr. Osborne and Mr. Wesker start out with much the same ideology ('If you don't care, you'll die'), but that what emerges from the plays is radically different. My argument is that *Roots* achieves what *Look Back in Anger* might have achieved, but in fact only promises."

3. Popkin, "Jewish Writers in England," *Commentary* (February, 1961), p. 139.

4. *Ibid.*

5. *Ibid.*

6. Leftwich, "Anglo-Jewish Literature," *The Jewish Quarterly* (London: Spring, 1953). Reprinted in *Caravan*, edited by Jacob Sonntag (New York and London, 1962).

7. "Jewishness in Today's Writers," *Jewish Chronicle* (London: November 4, 1960).

8. Wesker, "A Crucial Question," *The Jewish Quarterly* (London: Autumn, 1960), pp. 43-45.

9. Charles, "Trends in Anglo-Jewish Writing," *The Jewish Quarterly* (London: Spring, 1963), pp. 11-12.

Chapter Twelve

1. Jill Pomerance, in "Question and Answer," with Wesker's byline, *New Theatre Magazine*, published by the Green Room Society of the Drama Department of the University of Bristol, in the April, 1960 issue.

2. *Ibid*, p. 8.

3. *Ibid.*

4. *Ibid.*

5. In a letter to *New Statesman* (London: February 28, 1959), p. 293.

6. Winegarten, "Arnold Wesker: Is Sincerity Enough?", *Jewish Observer and Middle East Review* (London: April 19, 1963).

7. *Ibid.*, p. 18.

8. *Ibid.*

9. *Ibid.*

10. *Ibid.*, p.19.

11. Gellert, "Chips and After," *New Statesman* (London: May 11, 1962), p. 685.

12. *Ibid.*

13. *Ibid.*

14. Pritchett, "A World of Kitchens," *New Statesman* (London: July 7, 1961), p.24.

15. *Ibid.*

16. *Ibid.*

17. *Ibid.*

18. Rosselli, "The Wesker Twist," *The Reporter* (September 13, 1962), p. 52.

19. *Ibid.*

20. Jones, "The Theatre of Arnold Wesker," *The Critical Quarterly* (London: Winter, 1960).

21. *Ibid.*

22. Beavan, "Missionary in the Theatre," *The New York Times Magazine* (October 13, 1963), pp. 28, 73, 74, 76, 78.

23. Morton Gottlieb.

24. In 1963 *Chicken Soup with Barley* was performed in Bologna and in Milan. Sandro D'Amico reported on the Italian performances in *The London Magazine* (October, 963), pp. 72-73. Discussing the Bologna version, in Italian, of course, D'Amico said, "The critics praised the performance unreservedly, but the public was left cold. Thus on both fronts the very things the organizers of the new *teatro stabile* were hoping to arouse—discussion and controversy—were missing. Why? Probably because Puecher [Virginio Puecher, its director] interpreted Wesker's realism in strictly naturalistic terms, concentrating wholly on atmosphere, on states of mind, and on all the elements that were moving and affecting in the play. An over-subtle psychology and insufficiently incisive. I think that if one were trying to stir up public opinion, emphasizing the text's strong polemical potential, a more lucid and, at points, symbolical performance would have been needed; one in which stress was laid on the narration of events rather than on the psychology of the characters." In other words, the social and political issues would have been more interesting to the Italian audience than the character delineation. An interesting observation. The audience, D'Amico reports, saw "a fatalistic, rather than a socialist, play."

25. The information on the countries in which foreign rights were sold was given to me by Wesker and his agent. In Germany *Chicken Soup with Barley* was bought by the publishing firm of Fischer Verlag, which also purchased *Roots*, *I'm Talking About Jerusalem*, *The*

Kitchen, and *Chips with Everything*. In Germany, too, some of Wesker's plays have been performed: *Chicken Soup with Barley, Roots,* and *I'm Talking About Jerusalem. Roots* was also staged in Holland, *The Kitchen* in Rotterdam, and *Chips with Everything* in Antwerp. The publisher Hans Keuls bought the rights to *Roots, The Kitchen,* and *Chips with Everything*. This information, which includes the entire listing of foreign rights sold, came in a letter dated January 31, 1964, from Wesker, with the list compiled by his agent.

26. Taylor, *Anger and After,* both in the English Penguin and in the American edition published in Baltimore. The English hardcover edition of this volume is entitled *The Angry Theatre*. Some of the other volumes in which Wesker's work is treated can be found in the bibliography.

27. His latest plays, not yet in production, are *Their Very Own and Golden City* and *The Four Seasons*.

28. Wesker, "Art—Therapy or Experience," *Views No. 4* (London: Spring, 1964), pp. 44-47.

29. *Ibid.,* p. 44.

30. *Ibid.,* p. 47.

Selected Bibliography

PRIMARY SOURCES

The Hill. London: *The Jewish Quarterly* (Autumn, 1958). A short story.
Pools. London: *The Jewish Quarterly* (Winter, 1958-1959). Reprinted in *Caravan: A Jewish Quarterly Omnibus,* edited by Jacob Sonntag. New York and London: Thomas Yoseloff, 1962. Pp. 160-84. A short story.
Chicken Soup with Barley. New English Dramatists 1. Three plays introduced and edited by E. Martin Browne. Harmondsworth, Middlesex: Penguin Books, 1959. The other two plays in this volume are *Each His Own Wilderness,* by Doris Lessing, and *The Hamlet of Stepney Green,* by Bernard Kops.
Roots. Harmondsworth, Middlesex: Penguin Books, 1959.
"Time Parts the Memory." London: *The Jewish Quarterly* (Winter, 1959-1960). Reprinted in *Caravan: A Jewish Quarterly Omnibus,* edited by Jacob Sonntag. A poem.
The Kitchen. New English Dramatists 2. Harmondsworth, Middlesex: Penguin Books, 1960. The other two plays in this volume are *A Resounding Tinkle,* by N. F. Simpson, and *Epitaph for George Dillon,* by John Osborne and Anthony Creighton.
The Wesker Trilogy. London: Jonathan Cape, 1960.
I'm Talking About Jerusalem. Harmondsworth, Middlesex: Penguin Books, 1960.
"Discovery." London and New York: *The Transatlantic Review* 5 (December, 1960), pp. 16-18. An autobiographical statement.
"A Crucial Question." London: *The Jewish Quarterly* (Autumn, 1960), 43-45. A review of Gerda Charles' *The Crossing Point.*
The Kitchen. New York: Random House, 1961.
"Art Is Not Enough." London: *The Twentieth Century* (February, 1961), pp. 190-94.
The Wesker Trilogy. New York: Random House, 1961.
The Kitchen. Rev. ed. London: Jonathan Cape, 1961.
"The Secret Reins." London: *Encounter* (March, 1962), p. 306. An

essay on the founding and the purpose of the Centre 42 movement.

Chips with Everything. London: Jonathan Cape, 1962.

Chips with Everything. New York: Random House, 1962.

Chips with Everything. London: *Plays and Players* (December, 1962).

The Menace. London: *The Jewish Quarterly* (Spring, 1963). The first version of an original television play.

"Director's Introduction to the Report." *Annual Report 1961-1962 Fortytwo.* Published by Centre 42 Ltd., 20 Fitzroy Square, London. Pp. 2-5.

"Wesker on 42." London: *The Observer Weekend Review* (July 7, 1963), p. 19. An extract from Mr. Wesker's introduction to the first annual report of Centre 42.

"Centre 42." London: *The Way* (October, 1963), p. 8. An essay in which Mr. Wesker calls upon the working man to aid Centre 42.

Chips with Everything. New English Dramatists 7. Harmondsworth, Middlesex: Penguin Books, 1963. The other plays included in this volume are *Afore Night Come,* by David Rudkin, and *Everything in the Garden,* by Giles Cooper.

Chips with Everything. Theatre Arts (October, 1963), pp. 35-57.

"Art—Therapy or Experience." London: *Views No. 4* (Spring, 1964), pp. 44-47.

The Wesker Trilogy. Harmondsworth, Middlesex: Penguin Books, 1964.

The Kitchen. Harmondsworth, Middlesex: Penguin Books, 1964. The two additional dramas in this volume are *Epitaph for George Dillon,* by John Osborne and Anthony Creighton, and *The Hamlet of Stepney Green,* by Bernard Kops.

Roots. In *The New British Drama,* edited and with an introduction by Henry Popkin. New York: Grove Press, 1964. This collection includes five other British plays, plus an essay by Arnold Wesker, "Let Battle Commence."

Chips with Everything. In *The Best Plays 1963-1964,* edited by Henry Hewes. New York: Dodd, Mead, 1964. A condensed version of the play is included in this, the forty-sixth volume of an annual series of major plays performed each year in the United States.

SECONDARY SOURCES

I. Criticism

ALLEN, WALTER. *Some Post-War British Writers.* Denmark: Sveriges Radio, 1963. A collection of radio talks by a well-known British

critic. In the chapter on Wesker, Mr. Allen stresses the Wesker
Trilogy. "Wesker," he says, "seems to be reviving a tradition of
British socialism one had long thought dead, that associated par-
ticularly with the great nineteenth-century poet-artist-craftsman,
William Morris."

AMIS, KINGSLEY. "Not Talking About Jerusalem," *The Spectator* (London: August, 10, 1962), p.190. In reviewing the published versions of all of Wesker's plays, Mr. Amis admits that he has seen
none of the dramas on stage, but says that he has read them
and dislikes them all.

BALLIETT, WHITNEY. "Maybe," *The New Yorker* (March 18, 1961),
pp. 126-27. This is a violently negative critique of *Roots*. Mr.
Balliett labels it as "a static, fallen-arches attempt to record,
through dialect speech and an endless series of pale, enlarged,
still-photograph scenes, the day-to-day life in Norfolk of a dull,
poor, and ignorant family of laborers and farmers."

BRIEN, ALAN. "Theatre, London," *Theatre Arts* (December, 1959),
pp. 20, 22. A report on new plays in London, with high praise
for *Roots*. "Arnold Wesker," Mr. Brien writes, "has brilliantly
caught the idiomatic rhythms of the speech. . . . Excitingly and
movingly and comically, he reproduces not only the surface erup-
tions of humor and anger but also the banked fires that glow
beneath."

BROWNE, E. MARTIN. "Theatre Survey," *Drama Survey* (London:
October, 1962), p. 183. A studious report on the contemporary
British theater, with kind words for Wesker and regret that he
decided to give so much time to Centre 42.

BRUSTEIN, ROBERT. "Fragments From a Cultural Explosion," *The
New Republic* (March 27, 1961), p. 30. Mr. Brustein has mixed
feelings about *Roots*. "Compared with Albee," he informs us,
Wesker "looks like a theatrical primitive." Yet he takes Wesker
seriously. "It is easy to dismiss this piece as boring and banal,
but it is written with such overwhelming sincerity that one is
somehow prevented from a final judgment. Actually, *Roots*—
gagged as it is by mindless characters—is the weakest play in the
Chicken Soup trilogy. In the other two works, Wesker has more
complexity about politics and human nature, and proves, if not
more artful than Albee, then certainly less self-indulgent."

———. "The Backwards Birds," *The New Republic* (October 19,
1963), pp. 28, 30-31. This is an extended review of both John Osborne's *Luther* and Wesker's *Chips with Everything*. Mr. Brustein writes that "Wesker is animated by a profound political faith
which gives him emotional intensity at the expense of artistic

finish; his plays are always threatening to fall into socialist propaganda. *Chips with Everything* is no exception, but it has been vitally enhanced by an interesting military setting, and a superb production by the English Stage Company."

CHAPMAN, JOHN. " 'Chips with Everything' Strong, Penetrating, Crisp, Well Staged," *New York Daily News* (October 2, 1963), p. 64. A favorable notice by an influential reviewer, who calls *Chips with Everything* "a good, vigorous, masculine import."

————. "Two Strong New Dramas: 'Luther' and 'Chips With,' " *Sunday News* (October 20, 1963), Section Two, p. 1. Mr. Chapman reconsiders two English imports and repeats his praise of the Wesker play, and of the Osborne drama. On the Wesker effort, he writes, "This is an absorbing, splendidly staged play, and it is earthy and funny in its details."

"Chips with Everything," *Plays and Players* (London: July, 1962), pp. 20-23, 50. Reviews of the play as it was produced in London, Sheffield, and Glasgow, by Peter Roberts, Eric Chapman, and Peter Hamilton. Geoffrey Ost, director of the Sheffield Playhouse, and Callum Mill, director of the Glasgow Citizens' group that mounted the play, analyze their production problems.

CLURMAN, HAROLD. "Theatre," *The Nation* (October 26, 1963), pp. 267-68. A noted director and drama critic makes the interesting point that *"Chips with Everything* gives evidence of its author's genuine struggle with his material, a struggle with himself as well as with his community."

COHEN, MARK. "The World of Wesker," *The Jewish Quarterly* (London: Winter, 1960-1961), p. 45. A review of the published versions of *The Wesker Trilogy* and *The Kitchen,* lucid and illuminating.

————. "Impersonal Hero," *The Jewish Quarterly* (London: Autumn, 1962), pp. 48-49. A review of the published version of *Chips with Everything.* Cohen sees power in the play but says that it ultimately fails as a personal tragedy although it could "hardly be bettered" as a social drama.

COLEMAN, ROBERT. " 'Chips' Is Amusing, Moving," *New York Mirror* (October 2, 1963), p. 31. In his notice of *Chips with Everything* Mr. Coleman says that the tense drama "kept the Plymouth Theatre first-nighters on the edge of their seats." He adds that "Wesker can write. He has a sense of the dramatic and a flair for comedy. . . . He knows how to move masses of men about a stage, and spotlight the problems of individuals among them with fluidity."

Selected Bibliography

DENNIS, NIGEL. "What Though the Field Be Lost?" *Encounter* (London: August, 1962), pp. 43-45. A brilliant critical study of *Chips with Everything,* which explains why it is so impressive to the British theatergoer and why its impact is so deep.

FINDLATER, RICHARD. "Plays and Politics," *The Twentieth Century* (London: September, 1960), pp. 235-41. An incisive analysis of Wesker's themes and his political views.

"A Fine Dish," *Newsweek* (October 14, 1963), p. 72. On the New York production of *Chips with Everything,* the *Newsweek* critic writes, "Inside a shell of realism, Wesker has written a tractarian fantasy in which all the characters are emblems of a social conflict alien to this country. Yet their loaded interplay has a stinging immediacy in the theatre which must be something like the effect of the young Clifford Odets a quarter of a century ago."

FRASER, G. S. *The Modern Writer and His World.* Baltimore: Penguin Books, 1964. In a chapter entitled "The Wind of Change in the 1950s" Fraser analyzes all of Wesker's work and finds him "a much more politically and intellectually articulate and committed dramatist than Osborne, but much more naive (or naive in a different way) as a person and craftsman. . . . I think he has the potentiality of being something more than a latter-day Galsworthy. . . ."

GASCOIGNE, BAMBER. "Goodbye, Mr. Chips," *The Spectator* (London: May, 11, 1962), p. 621. *The Spectator*'s critic writes a scathing notice of *Chips with Everything,* declaring that it makes "Wesker's already over-simplified sociology appear quite grotesque."

GELLERT, ROGER. "Chips and After," *New Statesman* (London: May 11, 1962), p. 685. In a critique on the British production of *Chips with Everything,* Mr. Gellert claims that "Wesker has got away from Jewishness and politics, and shows a sympathetic and subtle understanding of class tensions and the stranglehold of Authority."

HATCH, ROBERT. "Arise, Ye Playgoers of the World," *Horizon* (July, 1961), pp. 116-18. An analysis of Edward Albee's short plays and Wesker's *Roots.* Mr. Hatch says of *Roots* that it "goes on ringing in my ears as few plays have recently."

————. "Theatre," *The Nation* (March 25, 1961), p. 272. In a brief but provocative review of *Roots,* Mr. Hatch correctly reports that Wesker's people are rootless in the sense that they have been cut off where they stand, their traditions atrophied beneath them and their lives rotting. He is in effect calling on the British masses to rouse themselves from a sleep that is sliding toward death: our rootlessness induces intoxication rather than somnolence."

HEWES, HENRY. "Keep the Home Fires Frying," *Saturday Review* (October 19, 1963), p. 30. According to Mr. Hewes, "While *Chips with Everything* is in some respects a loaded thesis play, it is also honest in that the author has set down with accuracy and insight a milieu of which he himself has been a part."

JONES, A. R. "The Theatre of Arnold Wesker," *The Critical Quarterly* (London: Winter, 1960). A highly laudatory essay on Wesker's art, closely reasoned and eloquently phrased. "Wesker," Mr. Jones writes, "has rewritten the myth of our time and rewritten it from the point of view of those who suffered and, somehow survived the crises and disillusionments of the last twenty-five years."

KERR, WALTER. "Chips with Everything," *New York Herald Tribune* (October 2, 1963), p. 18. Mr. Kerr, in his review of the Broadway production of *Chips with Everything,* praises the play: "The author puts together a kind of Living Newspaper style that everywhere, and with energy, speaks his mind. The evening may have something of a graph's coolness; but it is ruler-trim and lands with a slap. If it is probably a bit cooler here, emotionally speaking, than it was in Britain, the cause is no doubt to be found in our obvious social differences (I did not say advantages). The reconciliation is undoubtedly moving on home territory; American audiences are less likely to feel themselves immediately involved."

————. "Magic Over Matter," *New York,* The Sunday *Herald Tribune* Magazine (October 27, 1963), p. 25. An analysis of four plays of the season, including *Chips with Everything,* which Mr. Kerr continues to find "surprisingly agreeable."

LEECH, CLIFFORD. "Two Romantics: Arnold Wesker and Harold Pinter," in *Contemporary Theatre,* (Stratford-Upon-Avon Studies 4, general editors John Russell Brown and Bernard Harris). New York: St. Martin's Press, 1962. A study of two of England's leading playwrights who "have quickly become known as possessing talent and integrity and promise." They are "complementary dramatists, different in technique, in the nature of their skills, in the attitudes towards humanity that their plays exhibit." Favorable treatment of both dramatists.

LEWIS, EMORY. "Chips with Everything," *Cue* (October 12, 1963), p. 15. Here is a short but unqualified rave review of the Broadway production of *Chips with Everything:* "Arnold Wesker's London hit is theatre incandescence of the highest power, one of the best plays of the decade. Ex-pastry cook Wesker, a mere thirty-one, emerges as a major twentieth-century dramatist. . . . Wesker's boys are no mere pegs for an author's thesis. They are very much alive, and involved in complex relationships each with the other as well as in broader class cleavages."

McCLAIN, JOHN. "Lively Play About RAF," *New York Journal-American* (October 2, 1963), p. 27. A mixed view on *Chips with Everything*. Mr. McClain appreciates the play's humor and liveliness and adds that it is a generally fascinating experience, even though it does not quite ring true. I was impatient with the boy for his stupid stand against a tradition he isn't going to beat, and I never for a minute believed in the attitudes of his commanding officers."

McGUINESS, FRANK. "Culture With Chips," *The London Magazine* (London: July, 1962), pp. 48-50. Mr. McGuiness is *not* on Wesker's side and does not care for any of his work. He considers Wesker to be the spokesman of "the chic anti-Establishment." In this bitter, but amusingly written attack, Mr. McGuiness observes: "Indeed, without stretching my fancy to breaking point, I could almost imagine that for the lunatic fringe of the audience I sat with the other evening [at a performance of *Chips with Everything*], to criticize Wesker as a dramatist would appear little less than a piece of sacrilegious impertinence, rather as if one were to judge Christ on his merits as a carpenter." Mr. McGuiness calls the play "the most arrogant, misconceived, simple-minded piece of proselytizing burlesque that it has been my misfortune to grip the edge of my seat through."

MANDER, JOHN. *The Writer and Commitment*. Philadelphia: Dufour Editions, 1962. Mr. Mander is especially good on Wesker's political and social commitment as he writes in depth about *Roots* and makes passing references to other Wesker dramas. He also lingers on Osborne's Jimmy Porter in *Look Back in Anger*.

MARRIOTT, R. B. "Chips With Everything Is Wesker's Best . . ." *The Stage and Television Today* (London: May 3, 1962), p. 13. This play, Mr. Marriott insists, "is Mr. Wesker's best play, an advance in every respect on all his other work, and one of the most valuable and absorbing plays to be seen at the Court since John Osborne took the stage there."

NADEL, NORMAN. "Chips Has Everything," *New York World-Telegram and Sun* (October 2, 1963), p. 41. Mr. Nadel writes: "Mr. Wesker, with director John Dexter and all hands, has brought us a clean play, a tidy play. It is a play that shapes up, secures itself and passes inspection like the conscripts themselves, standing at present arms in the stirring final moment."

PANTER-DOWNES, MOLLIE. "Letter from London," *The New Yorker* (May 12, 1962), pp. 160, 163. Writing on a variety of subjects,

Mrs. Panter-Downes reports on the London performances of *Chips with Everything* and remarks that "the play's total effect as a furious anti-Establishment attack . . . is devastating."

POPKIN, HENRY. "Class War With Everything," *The New Leader* (October 28, 1963), pp. 31, 32. The action comes off well in *Chips with Everything*, according to Mr. Popkin, but the human relationships are awkward and embarrassing. "Wesker too insistently sees himself as a part of the class war, and so he cannot see the rest of it for the purposes of his play." (The "it" is the "eye of the storm.")

PRYCE-JONES, ALAN. "Alan Pryce-Jones at the Theatre," *Theatre Arts* (May, 1961), p. 56. In a survey of a handful of dramas, the British writer is brief but pointed about *Roots*, which he calls "a play of ideas rather than action. Partly it is a critique of socialism written from the inside."

RIBALOW, HAROLD U. "The Plays of Arnold Wesker," *Chicago Jewish Forum* (Winter, 1962-63), pp. 127-31. A study of *The Wesker Trilogy* and *The Kitchen*, including background material on the original characters of Dave and Ada in *I'm Talking About Jerusalem*.

"Roots." *Time* (March 17, 1961), p. 42. *Time*'s reviewer charges that *Roots* is not a strong play because "Wesker uses a slice-of-life technique to convey a slice of lifelessness," but he adds that "in a theater season of flaccid falsity, there is something to respect in the way it rings true."

ROSSELLI, JOHN. "The Wesker Twist," *The Reporter* (September 13, 1962), pp. 48-51. Mr. Rosselli, writing from London, calls *Chips with Everything* "the most exciting piece of theatre in London just now," and proceeds to list its strengths and weaknesses.

"Sheep That Don't Say Baa." *Time* (October 11, 1963), pp. 72-73. On *Chips with Everything*. The anonymous *Time* critic is inclined to praise the play: "Wesker's chip is on his shoulder, and in heavier hands his play might have been doctrinaire agitprop-wash. It escapes that dreary fate, thanks to the playwright's good humor, dramatic interplay and irony, together with Director John Dexter's drillmasterly pacing. It is, in its own lingo, a scorching fine evening of theatre."

SIGAL, CLANCY. "Chips with Everything," *Queen* (London: May 15, 1962), p. 10. Mr. Sigal calls this play Wesker's "toughest, most pessimistic play" and the playwright "a moral thermometer for the rest of us."

SMITH, MICHAEL. "Wesker's 'Chips,'" *The Village Voice* (October 10, 1963), pp. 15, 18-19. Conceding that *Chips with Everything* is "very good theatre," Mr. Smith expresses his reservations about it: "Wesker, who like it or not is a member of the intelligentsia, has the folksy, condescending fondness for the lower classes that was until recently reserved in this country for well-behaved Negroes . . ."

SPENCER, CHARLES. "Arnold Wesker as a Playwright," *The Jewish Quarterly* (London: Winter, 1959-1960), pp. 40-41. Warm praise for the "seriousness and eloquence" of *Chicken Soup with Barley* and *Roots*.

TAUBMAN, HOWARD. "Life with R.A.F. Trainees," *New York Times* (October 2, 1963), p. 49. In an admiring review, Mr. Taubman recommends *Chips with Everything* and says of Wesker that "the young British playwright has more on his mind than an account of the fun and games and the pains of conscripts in the peacetime R.A.F. As a man who has made no secret of his socialist convictions, he has mounted a fierce attack not simply on the military mind and its brutalizing influence but also on the British class system."

TAYLOR, JOHN RUSSELL. *The Angry Theatre. New British Drama.* New York: Hill and Wang, 1962. The best single volume yet written about the modern British theater, although Taylor seems to wish to argue with Wesker. A Pelican paperback reprint, published in the United States in 1964 as *Anger and After*, contains additional material by the author and an analysis of *Chips with Everything*.

———. "Arnold Wesker," *The Times* (London: December 12, 1963). An unsigned piece, which Taylor sent to me. Taylor calls Wesker a "committed artist," and interviews him skillfully on his more recent views. Apparently Wesker would have liked to alter some of the dialogue in his earlier work and talked at length about his newest play, not yet produced when the interview took place, and when this manuscript was prepared. Wesker calls his latest effort more complex than his earlier work and, according to Taylor, "has come a long way from the simple realism of *Chicken Soup with Barley*."

———. "Mr. Wesker's 'Menace,'" *The Listener* (London: December 12, 1963), p. 1001. Admitting that his "lack of sympathy" with Wesker is "quite notorious," in this review of Wesker's television play, Mr. Taylor declares: "I liked his new play . . . better than anything else he has written. . . . If this is what television brings out in him one can only hope that it will not be long before he tackles the medium again. . . ."

TYNAN, KENNETH. "The Chip and the Shoulder," *The Observer* (London: May 6, 1962). Mr. Tynan calls *Chips with Everything* "furious, compassionate and unforgiving." He praises Wesker's "good ear" and "a shaping mind and a remarkable flair for character-revealing rhythms."

WATTS, RICHARD, JR. "Another Striking British Drama," *New York Post* (October 2, 1963), p. 68. *Chips with Everything* "could no doubt be described as left-wing 'propaganda,' but it is never done in terms of soapbox editorializing. Presenting its case with skillful theatrical effectiveness, it is a drama of striking power, intensity and conviction."

――――. "Paradox in 'Chips with Everything,'" *New York Post* (October 20, 1963), p. 15. Reflecting on the success in the United States of *Chips with Everything*, Mr. Watts, in a follow-up essay on his initial review, feels that American audiences misunderstood the play; they missed the bitterness in the humor and some critics thought the conclusion was "a shameless example of proud British flagwaving" instead of an indictment of R.A.F. authoritarianism.

WINEGARTEN, RENEE. "Arnold Wesker: Is Sincerity Enough?" *Jewish Observer and Middle East Review* (London: April 19, 1963), pp. 18-19. In a review of Wesker's published plays the critic writes that it is Wesker's head, not his heart, which "lets him down." He believes that "Wesker takes no account of the complexity and corruption of human nature, its convolutions, its hidden abysses. He does not face the fact that human beings, regardless of birth and class, are a tissue of incoherence and inconsistency."

WELLWARTH, GEORGE E. *The Theatre of Protest and Paradox.* New York: New York University Press, 1964. In a chapter entitled " 'Awake and Sing' in Whitechapel," Mr. Wellwarth judges all of Wesker's work and finds it lacking in skill and importance. He believes that "Wesker has never been able to rid himself of the deep-seated inferiority complex he seems to have developed as a result of being born into the working classes." Mr. Wellwarth fails to understand why the British critics consider Wesker an important dramatist.

II. Background Material

ALLSOP, KENNETH. *The Angry Decade.* New York: British Book Centre, 1958. A critical survey of the British writers of the 1950's, including Kingsley Amis, Colin Wilson, John Osborne, John Wain, and Nigel Dennis. It is an opinionated, lively work.

Selected Bibliography

"Arnold Wesker," *Current Biography* (February, 1962), pp. 43-45. A detailed and important account of Wesker's life and work. It contains some minor errors but it is in the main accurate.

BEAVAN, JOHN. "Missionary in the Theatre," *The New York Times Magazine* (October 13, 1963), pp. 28, 73, 74, 76, 78. Writing from London following the success of *Chips with Everything* in New York, Mr. Beavan reports on Centre 42 and Wesker's "message" to the British people.

CHARLES, GERDA. "East and West," *The Jewish Quarterly* (London: Winter, 1960-1961), pp. 5-7. A review of the Jewish literary scene in England, with shrewd observations on Brian Glanville, Frederic Raphael, Arnold Wesker, Harold Pinter, Bernard Kops, and Peter Shaffer.

————. "Elizabethan Age of Modern Jewish Literature," *World Jewry* (London: September, 1961), pp. 15-17. Miss Charles describes the "Jewish breakthrough" into British literature during the decade of 1950-60. Making some references to American writers, she stresses the work of English-Jewish authors and compares Wesker with Paddy Chayefsky.

D'AMICO, SANDRO. "Theatre," *The London Magazine* (October, 1963), pp. 72-76. An interesting account of the contemporary stage in Italy, in which Mr. D'Amico tells us how Italians reacted to *Chicken Soup with Barley* in an Italian translation. The critics were warm; the public was cold.

DEXTER, JOHN. "Working with Arnold," *Plays and Players* (London: April, 1962), p. 11. Mr. Dexter, who has directed all of Wesker's dramas, writes on "five years of intensive collaboration" with the playwright and explains the degree of his own participation in each of Wesker's plays.

————. "Chips and Devotion," *Plays and Players* (London: December, 1962), p. 32. The director of *Chips with Everything* writes of his approach to the play, to Wesker, and to the company that made the drama successful.

"The Future of Centre 42," *Challenge* (London: October, 1963), p. 2. An unsigned interview with Wesker on Centre 42 and its financial difficulties.

GASCOIGNE, BAMBER. *Twentieth Century Drama*. London: Hutchinson and Co., 1962. A survey of the drama of the Twenties, Thirties, Forties, and Fifties, analyzing the style of the dramatists, and with special emphasis laid on the works of Pirandello, O'Neill, Brecht, Giraudoux, Anouilh, Sartre, Eliot, Tennessee Williams, and Arthur Miller. In a section on "The New Playwrights" Gascoigne briefly reviews Wesker's work and questions whether Wesker's "drama will be able to develop." He also compares Wesker with Odets.

GINDIN, JAMES. *Postwar British Fiction.* University of California Press, 1962. This study is about the entire contemporary British literary scene, with a section on the drama and a few perceptive pages on Wesker, who "uses political or social details to illustrate points about individuals."

HARTLEY, ANTHONY. *A State of England.* New York: Harcourt, Brace and World, Inc., 1963. Mr. Hartley, in his survey of modern and contemporary England, has some astute things to say about recent trends in his native land. In a chapter entitled "The Cultural Debate" he weighs the quality of British culture and faces up to the problem of "cultural transmission." In the course of his remarks, he discusses *Roots* and *Chips with Everything.*

KITCHIN, LAURENCE. *Mid-Century Drama.* London: Faber and Faber, 1960. Mr. Kitchin includes a series of his interviews (for the *Times* of London) with British playwrights, actors, and directors. The interview with Wesker is a valuable one.

KOPS, BERNARD. "The Young Writer and the Theatre," *The Jewish Quarterly* (London: Summer, 1961), pp. 19-22. Kops explains how his generation of playwrights has come to the forefront and what it is that he and other writers are attempting to convey.

———. *The World Is a Wedding.* New York: Coward-McCann, Inc., 1963. The playwright—author of *The Hamlet of Stepney Green, The Dream of Peter Mann,* and *Enter Solly Gold* (which was first produced by Centre 42)—tells of his life up to the time he wrote his initial drama. His autobiography is an arresting book and it describes, in part, the same East End from which Wesker emerged. Both men, when children, were sent to the country to escape the blitz on London, and Kops's account of Jewish family life resembles Wesker's chronicle in his Trilogy.

LEE, JENNIE. "Wesker's Centre 42," *Encounter* (London, August, 1962), pp. 95-96. A letter by the widow of Labour leader Aneurin Bevan, who is herself a member of Parliament, in which she pays tribute to Wesker for his faith and vision in accepting leadership in the Centre 42 movement.

MAROWITZ, CHARLES. "Oh Mother, Is It Worth It?", *Theatre Arts* (May, 1962), pp. 21-22, 72-73. A useful article on Centre 42, how it was established, what its aims are, and whether it can prove to be valuable to those who care for the theater.

POMERANCE, JILL. "Question and Answer," *New Theatre Magazine* (Bristol: April, 1960), pp. 5-8. An interview with Wesker in which he discusses, as of 1960, the dramatic scene and some of his contemporaries. The magazine is published by the Green Room Society of the Drama Department of The University of Bristol.

POPKIN, HENRY. "Jewish Writers in England," *Commentary* (February, 1961), pp. 135-41. Mr. Popkin describes the beginning of a new tradition in England and discusses the work of Wesker, Kops, Mankowitz, Gerda Charles, Glanville, and Raphael.

ROTHBERG, ABRAHAM. "Waiting for Wesker," *Antioch Review* (Winter, 1964-65), pp. 492-505. A perceptive interview with Wesker, primarily about Centre 42.

SPENCER, CHARLES S. "The New Generation of Anglo-Jewish Playwrights," in *Jewish Book Annual Volume 22*. New York: Jewish Book Council of America, 1964. A cursory and somewhat superficial essay on Pinter, Wesker, Kops, Shaffer, and earlier English-Jewish dramatists. The critic grants Wesker talent but states flatly, "Once he seeks to proselytize, his work fails."

SPENDER, STEPHEN. "A Literary Letter from London," *The New York Times Book Review* (November 20, 1960), pp. 74-75. A noted British poet and editor of *Encounter* analyzes the modern English literary scene and makes some pertinent references to the Wesker influence.

TAYLOR, JOHN RUSSELL. "British Theatre," in *On Contemporary Literature*, edited by Richard Kostelanetz. New York: Avon Books, 1964. A useful survey article on the British drama from 1956 to 1962. Wesker's Trilogy, Taylor says, and his other plays, "make a number of worthwhile points clumsily."

THOMPSON, DENNIS. "British Experiment in Art for the Masses," *New Republic* (November 21, 1964), pp. 7-8. In a report on Centre 42 the writer states that "Wesker has made remarkable progress, and his experiment promises to be, at the least, an instructive experiment in mass culture."

TRILLING, OSSIA. "The New English Realism," *Tulane Drama Review* (Winter, 1962), pp. 184-93. In surveying the contemporary British stage, Mr. Trilling emphasizes the Centre 42 movement and makes some good observations on *Chips with Everything*.

WARDLE, IRVING. "New Waves on the British Stage," *Twentieth Century* (London: Summer, 1963); reprinted in *Plays and Players* (London: October, 1963), pp. 12-14. A discussion on the "angry young men" of the English stage, their upsurge and decline, and their persistence, with special reference to Osborne, Wesker, Delaney, Behan, and Kops.

————. "Revolt Against the West End," *Horizon* (January, 1963), pp. 26-33. A report on the activities, achievements, successes, and failures of the Royal Court Theatre, where "a company of young rebels has broken with a genteel tradition in the name of defiant realism and experiment." Wardle discusses Osborne, Nigel Dennis, N. F. Simpson, John Arden, Harold Pinter, and Arnold Wesker.

WERSHBA, JOSEPH. "A Cultural Rebel," *New York Post* (October 28, 1963). An interview with Wesker, in which the dramatist talks of his background and his battle against mediocrity.

"Wesker on 42," *The Observer Weekend Review* (London: July 14, 1963), p. 22. In response to Wesker's article a week earlier—drawn from the Centre 42 annual report—four influential Englishmen offer their reactions to Centre 42. They are George Woodcock, General Secretary of the Trades Union Congress; Clive Jenkins, General Secretary of The Association of Supervisory Staffs, Executives and Technicians; George Devine, Artistic Director of the English Stage Company; and Bamber Gascoigne, theater critic of *The Observer*.

WILLIAMS, RAYMOND. "Recent English Drama, in *The Modern Age 7. The Pelican Guide to English Literature*, edited by Boris Ford. Baltimore: Pelican Books, 1963. A compressed but clear survey, in which Mr. Williams, a lecturer in English at the University of Cambridge, analyzes, in summary form, the work of Osborne, Delaney, Kops, Wesker, and others. He stresses their "bitter, almost inarticulate rage at the general condition."

WILSON, SHEILA. *The Theatre of the 'Fifties*. Foreword by Arnold Wesker. The Library Association. 1963. This is a booklist, a British bibliographical study of "essential reference books and periodical material for the student of the theatre." It includes material on acting and actors; on criticism; on television, radio, school, and religious drama. There are special listings on theater in Great Britain, Australia, France, Germany, Italy, Russia, and the United States, and on "world theatre," including eighteen other countries, among which are Austria, Finland, Greece, Israel, Sweden, Spain, Norway, Denmark, and Poland.

Index

Kitchen, The, 5, 25, 26, 28-33, 35, 39, 48, 58, 59, 113, 115, 116, 118, 119; *Kitchen, The* (film), 5, 6, 26, 28, 58; *Menace,* 94-96; *Pools,* 91-94; *Roots,* 5, 24, 26, 34, 35, 36, 37, 40, 41, 42-51, 52, 60, 85, 93, 96, 97, 98, 99, 108, 109, 113, 115, 116, 118, 119; *Their Very Own and Golden City,* 6, 7, 76-84, 85, 90, 119; *Chicken Soup with Barley, Roots, I'm Talking About Jerusalem,* referred to as Wesker trilogy, 5, 7, 8, 34, 36, 41, 42, 48, 52, 57, 59, 66, 116, 117, 120

Wesker, Joseph (Arnold Wesker's father), 25
Wesker, Leah (Perlmutter) (Arnold Wesker's mother), 25
Whiting, John, 102
Who's Afraid of Virginia Woolf? (Albee), 90
Williams, Tennessee, 74, 90, 114
Winegarten, Renee, 114, 115
Within and Without (Harvey), 22
World Is a Wedding, The (Kops), 25, 123
World War II, 53, 55
Wouk, Herman, 111

Zangwill, Israel, 108